THE
HOUSE-
HUSBAND'S
WORLD

THE HOUSE-HUSBAND'S WORLD

REFLECTIONS OF A FORMER DIPLOMAT-AT HOME

HAKON TORJESEN

THE GARDEN, Eden Prairie, Minnesota

Published by The Garden
P.O. Box 844, Eden Prairie, Minnesota 55344

Library of Congress Catalog Card No. 79-88302
International Standard Book No. 0-9602790-0-8
First Printing, May 1979

Printed in the United States of America
Cover design: Cathleen Casey

About the Author

Hakon Torjesen has been a househusband since 1972, when he and his wife, Karen Olness, agreed to switch family roles and embark on what they called "her decade" for a career. She teaches pediatrics.

They had spent the first ten years of their marriage in the U.S. foreign service, where he served with the U.S. Information Agency in Vientiane, Laos; Nairobi, Kenya; and Washington, D.C.

Hakon Torjesen was born in Norway and spent his childhood in China, where his parents were missionaries. He attended a British boarding school in China, and lived three years in a Japanese prison camp before immigrating to the United States in 1946. A graduate of the University of Minnesota, he became a radio journalist, and hosted a program called "Open Mike" on WCCO in Minneapolis.

The Torjesens have four children, aged 10, 11, 12 and 13. They live on a hobby farm in Eden Prairie, Minnesota, where they raise apples, nursery stock and raspberries. When not homemaking or farming, Hakon Torjesen's diversions include carpentry and writing. But his favorite hobby, as he explains in this book, is to daydream.

Acknowledgements

I am indebted to Erik, Kristine, Malika, Mark, and their mother, Karen, for being the family setting in which these ideas grew, and for surviving those winters when their homemaker was preoccupied with this manuscript.

Others who have read drafts and offered criticism include Kari and Bob Malcolm, Bruce and Vicky Lansky, Nancy Agneberg, Elisabeth Emerson, Rick Carlson, Mulford Q. Sibley, Kent Garborg, Gail Farber, Aaron and Jan Ament, Elsa Furst—and Charlie Fowler, who can spot a split infinitive at ten paces, but agreed to spare some of my cadences.

Quotations from the Bible are from Today's English Version, copyright by the American Bible Society, or from the oral tradition, mostly in the King James text.

To Karen

Contents

Introduction

On occasion over the past seven years, friends have asked when I will write my tale about being a househusband.

"I'm busy enough raising four kids," I would say.

"Besides," I could add, "the story isn't about being a househusband."

The story has to do with people exploring nicer ways to live and think in an advanced technological society. Every step of such an exploration brings surprises and opens new directions.

Our course led to my wife and me trading work roles; it presently finds her teaching pediatrics and all of us raising raspberries, apples and nursery stock on our ten acre "farm" in Eden Prairie, Minnesota. It also led us to finding some ways to simplify our lives and liking the result. We also felt ourselves attracted to broader interests—thoughts about our own values, our society's values, and about spiritual growth.

In the Mainstream

There is, I am told, something poignant about people who in mid-life come upon new dimensions to the routine of their existence.

I'm also told they're insufferable.

But there do seem to be more of us, and more dimensions. Harried city dwellers are discovering simple rural living. Locked-in breadwinners and homemakers are finding choices in roles. Cynics are even discovering naivete. And orderly minds are grasping the plasticity of reality.

A mere decade ago alternative styles of living seemed to belong only on the fringes of our society. My thoughts of trading a career for homemaking or a hobby farm were no more than an occasional and irreverent dream.

But today, explorations of ways to live and think are being made across the whole stream of our culture. Househusbands find themselves giving talks to Rotarians and to traditional women's clubs. The media and social scientists would now portray my drudgery in the raspberry patch as an example of "voluntary simplicity," a mainstream phenomenon that has drawn on both traditional and counter-culture values.

Why Explore?

It can be hard to see much of a pattern in all this, except that the people involved seem happier. That in itself is a lovely design.

But I think there is more to it.

For one thing, most of the explorations seem to be in a direction away from the more complicated ways of living and thinking—toward simpler ways of doing the same thing. After centuries of growth by elaboration, we are rediscovering the option of growing toward simplicity.

12

It is like a burst of new meaning to the teaching of Jesus that "unless you change and become like little children you will never enter the kingdom of heaven."

Even more remarkable, I think, is that so many explorations, starting from so many places, seem to be ending up in the general area of an integration of our inner and outer realities.

For several centuries in the West, we have muted the "in here" of our existence—while science was giving us bursts of insight into the "out there."

Now we seem to be rediscovering the ancient wisdom of acknowledging the connection between our internal and external states, and this awareness has emerged as the principle theme to many of the explorations of life and thought style in our day.

Enough of us are now prospecting these hills, and finding occasional nuggets, to suggest that we may be involved in some sort of "westward expansion" of consciousness.

Is this a renaissance? The last time our civilization rated that label it was after a revival of ancient classical tradition, which nourished a new wisdom. I suspect the label will fit this time, too.

A Datum

This book offers an outline of one middle-American mind at what seems to be a pregnant moment in our civilization.

Hopefully, this will be of some value to my "fellow gestators."

Hopefully, too, it will be fun. The experience of change was light-hearted, compared to its anticipation.

And I found myself exploring unexpected corners of life style and thought style.

These essays grew in the raspberry patch. It was quiet out there, so mental conversation tended to flow easily. Sometimes it was just chatter. But at other times the silence and the repetitive labor stilled my mind, and it spoke more clearly.

The exploration is still in progress, and could change direction tomorrow. Where it stands today is like a datum. It does not prove anything. But sometimes a datum can be a more useful sort of information than lots of data.

The exploration opens on the theme of househusbandry—and ends at the present limits of a personal search for a link between the inner and outer aspects of our realities.

En route, the chapters explore such terrain as the appeal of simpler life styles—and the decline of our public and private sectors in favor of an inner sector. An energy blessing is discovered where early maps had shown a crisis.

In each probe—from trying to learn about parenting to understanding the decade I spent in the foreign service—the key turns out to be the link between the internal and external states.

Background

Herewith some personal background:

Karen Olness, my wife, is a specimen Minnesota farm girl. She was reared without the mysteries of indoor plumbing, and she milked the cows every morning and night for seven years until the morning she left for the university wanting to become a doctor. She had reached that decision at age six. But she had never graced the inside of a physician's office until she filed her freshman application and was required to take a routine physical.

I am a typical immigrant, acting out the Great American Dream. My parents were Norwegian missionaries to China and sent their children to a British boarding school there. My father was killed in a World War II air raid when I was eleven. During my teens, our family spent three years in a Japanese concentration camp, where I learned that going slightly hungry much of the time is a thoroughly disagreeable way to live, but not as overwhelming in reality as it is in the abstract.

In the wave of displaced persons that came to America after the war, I followed a traditional path for my countrymen—starting in Brooklyn as a carpenter's apprentice, then moving to Minnesota to ride the American dream.

The dream sputtered characteristically, and eventually it soared. At times I wondered whether we were the last passengers. Then in the sixties the Cubans of Miami revived the dream again. And in the mid-seventies— when we thought it must surely have died—the refugees from Southeast Asia came to America and proved again that the dream was potent.

By the late fifties, having picked up a degree and dropped an accent, I had landed as a radio-journalist for WCCO in Minneapolis with a program called Open Mike. It caught the ear of the farm girl, by then working her way through medical school. I later went into press relations, and then to the staff of Minnesota Congressman Ancher Nelsen.

The immigrant in me marvelled in 1961 when I joined the foreign service with the U.S. Information Agency. We started our married life in Laos, and Karen volunteered as a missionary physician. In the mid-sixties we were back in Washington, where I headed the VOA Korean Service and Karen took a pediatric residency. We had our first-born. Then we returned to Laos.

This time we both had jobs in the U.S. mission, Karen as deputy director of the public health program, and I of the information program. Our second child was born and we adopted our third. We were fiercely busy and we were affluent.

Next we went to Nairobi, Kenya where I was press attache. It was my career that moved us; hers shrank into part-time and volunteer work.

Returning to Washington in the early seventies, we moved into a country house and vowed to stay put for awhile. But once again my wife had to settle for a part-time career. We began thinking that there might be nicer ways to live.

In 1972 we decided that my career decade had been a good one; now it would be "her decade" for a career. She joined the medical faculty at George Washington University, and I became a househusband. We adopted our fourth child. The brood I was husbanding now stood at ages 4, 5, 6 and 7.

In 1974 the new Minneapolis Children's Health Center asked Karen Olness to head its medical education and research program. The farm girl made a career move, returning to Minnesota complete with her supportive spouse and scrubbed kids.

The American dream was growing.

Part One

Exploring
Ways to Live

1
Househusbandry

In early 1972, a few weeks into my new life as a househusband, I was learning to cope with a rather typical domestic crisis. This one involved loading all the kids into the car for a tearful ride to the orthopedist's office, just in case that hurt arm of one of them was more serious than I thought. The receptionist was asking the routine questions.

Suddenly adrenalin roared through my body.

"And where do you work, sir?" she had asked.

I recovered in time to mutter that I was a financial consultant. This white lie was a gift from a thoughtful friend. He had worried about the male breadwinner stereotype in me and had signed me on as an unpaid vice-president of his small consulting firm, "just in case you ever need a title." I later thanked him for his insight, and ended up dabbling for a time in his business.

Fortunately, traumatic moments like that occurred only in the beginning. Soon it became a matter of choice to call myself a househusband. But there were other surprises to come.

"Her Decade"

Before trading roles Karen and I had soul-searched for a year or more about abandoning our traditional moorings. We realized that these moorings had been an assumption of our marriage from the start, that we were very close to being fixed in those initial roles—and liking it that way.

But we liked other things too. We wanted to pursue both our professions. We wanted a full family life. And we wanted, within safe limits, to increase our freedom of choice on how to live our lives.

In our first decade together we had tried makeshift accommodations to these wishes. But when it came time for me to transfer to a new post, my career would often cripple hers. And we found that, when we were both working full time, our lives became incredibly complicated, and our expenses and our standard of living quickly expanded to a point where we felt just as strapped as we would have on one income.

And there were the kids. They had a pediatrician for a mother who preferred, if at all possible, that preschoolers like they should receive their primary care from one of us, not from surrogates. And their father agreed. So one of us would have to continue subordinating a career to the obligations of a home.

There were other factors. Everyone who encountered her knew that Karen Olness had an extraordinary talent for her profession, one that deserved a primary career commitment.

For my part, I had cut a swath through several careers and could expect, in the normal course of breadwinning, that my frustrations would be on the increase and my stimulations on the decrease. I was ready for something new.

Fortunately, times were changing. By the early seventies it was becoming possible to consider the prospect of having a daddy concentrating on the home while mama pursued her career and brought in the mortgage and grocery money.

We concluded that, since my career had dominated the first decade of our marriage, we would now trade career roles. This was to be "her decade."

But what if her decade had been first? Obviously, our sequence of roles was the easy one, given the traditional norms in our society. It is not all that hard for a middle-aged man who has had a career and developed some measure of his identity to move out of a culturally assigned role. A young couple, starting their marriage in work roles traditionally assigned to the other sex, would have needed far more ego strength than what I mustered.

This, too, is changing, because our norms are changing. Soon our only fixed roles could be those assigned by biology: to sire or to bear. Beyond that, there's no predicting which family roles will first attract our sons and daughters. Hopefully, they will keep their options open—to choose, to share, and to live with diversity.

For our part, we felt relief, almost from the moment we cut loose, at having expanded on the rather narrow waters of our traditionally assigned roles in life. I wondered why it had taken me so long to learn that there could be more to the best years of a male in our society than a career outside the home.

New Roles

When we switched roles, the children were four, five and six years old—out of diapers, but still in that preschool stage where their care and feeding can demand most of a homemaker's day. And a year later we adopted our fourth child, who was then four.

It was not the sort of brood that lent itself to fulfilling the usual fantasy of trading roles so one could have more time for golf. Fortunately Karen, who has innate talent with children, remained deeply involved in the home—even as she immersed herself in her academic career at the medical school.

Both of us noted a cross-fertilization of styles in our new roles.

For example, Karen thought it would be a nice idea occasionally to bring one of the children along to spend a day with her at the office. So she did. Such an idea had not occurred to me during my decade, and I doubt whether it would have been accepted had I tried it. But before long Karen was noticing that her male colleagues would occasionally bring their children to the office too. Very nice!

Similarly, when I found myself spending close to an hour a day at the bottom of the driveway with sundry tots, waiting for nursery school and kindergarten buses, I reacted sensibly by installing a permanent lawnchair at curbside, where I could arrive with coffee and a book. My colleagues in adjoining driveways accepted all this with good grace—although I believe they would have taken less kindly to such irreverence from one of the mothers.

Diplomacy and Homemaking

What about the trivia of housework? It is awful! But my impression is that the scut work is fairly comparable to what you would find in most occupations.

An "in" box and a kitchen sink are about the same thing: devices for keeping used ideas or used dishes in circulation. Cleaning out either one is indisputably a trivial chore.

From having tasted both diplomacy and homemaking I've learned that there is an abundance of stimulation and of trivia in both concoctions, but I cannot name a clear winner in either category. I doubt whether people who have not worked in diplomacy or homemaking can understand the full measure of either their trivia or their stimulation.

Who but a homemaker would know that a large share of that job, so long as there are kids around, is a matter of chauffeuring?

And who would dream that diplomats spend most of their energies nursing the internal mechanism of a bureaucracy with little time left for matters of state?

Yet who, except one who has lived overseas, can comprehend the expansion of consciousness that can grow from extended exposure to something more than one's own culture? And working with the U.S. Information Agency, as I did, was one of the more intense forms of that experience, because U.S.I.A. dealt directly with the interactions between American perceptions and those of other cultures.

But seven years of trying to raise four children has humbled and stimulated me to the point where I now accept as gospel the old euphemism about parenting being the most demanding and most rewarding profession in the world. Fortunately, my wife wrote the book on parenting,* and happily her thesis is that the cacophony of advice from the experts is seldom as good as the answers we can develop for ourselves.

Identity

It started with the adoption of our fourth child.

I remember the furious cleaning under the beds that preceded our "home study" by a county social worker. No foreign service inspector had awed me as much as this dear soul, who was to determine whether the county could entrust a life to this . . . this . . . MAN!

The day we passed muster, I felt legitimate as a

---

*Karen Olness. *Raising Happy Healthy Children*, Meadowbrook Press, 1977.

househusband. The novelty of the role had worn off by then; and with the frustrations and feelings of inadequacy that surfaced, there was also growing in me a sense of satisfaction at being responsible for my children. I could identify now when, in a supermarket, I would see a young mother, in an unguarded moment, giggling with the child in her cart, or scolding the brat harshly.

A second event that helped sharpen my identity as a househusband was our move to Minnesota a few years later. In the Washington area our circle of friends came from earlier days and accepted me for my previous identity. Even my routine with the house and kids was inherited from their mother, and I had not made that many changes.

The role of a supportive spouse in a career move was one that my wife had played many times for me, and it was natural now to relish a chance to reciprocate. I experienced a vicarious thrill at seeing her opportunity for a career advancement develop. I even savored flying out with her in the recruiting process to be discreetly looked over by the search committee, much as I had checked out the appropriateness of foreign service wives in an earlier decade.

In Minnesota we built our friendships and our style of living on the premise that I was at home and Karen was working. And we felt comfortable.

Gradually, too, I began realizing something that I had not anticipated at the beginning of the decade. From having traded roles, I seemed to be expanding my identity rather than limiting it or threatening it.

Because I have now functioned as a breadwinner and a homemaker, I feel myself to be more than the sum of those parts, and to have gained insights into both the career world and the home world that I could not have found from playing only one or the other of those roles.

Chauvinism

I have tangled only with a most light-hearted variety of female chauvinism.

During my first year as a househusband, I was asked to volunteer at school as a "room mother"—which I did and enjoyed. Last year I was a "math mother" at an equally liberated suburban school. Year after year we have agreed that we are using these terms in their "generic sense," and that next year we'll stop using them.

In one school project I bore a distinction that boggled the former Rotarian in me—serving as a "Junior League Volunteer."

If there is any discrimination against househusbands, I seem to have missed it. Only rarely do I meet a male or female who feels threatened by my role. The more usual reaction, superficially at least, ranges from casual acceptance to admiration to envy.

If I happen to be in a feisty mood, it's easy to have some fun with the male stereotype. I recall from my early months as a househusband an all male business conference at an airport motel. The pressure was on to stay in session long enough to close the deal. But I wanted to stall. So I announced, "I can't miss that plane; I have to be home to cook supper." Within minutes the meeting adjourned in disarray.

There is, of course, something preposterous about the fuss that's made over househusbands. I can give speeches and write books about a field in which most of my colleagues are utterly ignored. And I have less experience than the average housewife. It reflects the overkill from our attempts at affirmative action. I suspect lady welders feel the same way. At a recent introductory lecture to twelve-year-olds in our school on the subject of careers, I found myself sharing the platform with a male nurse and a lady truck driver. Hardly a balanced view of careers!

Despite the distortions, though, it does seem to be getting easier for most of us in this culture to move into roles that were traditionally outside our spheres. Admittedly, explorers to some shores still tell us of restless natives. But the resistance is declining. And in the sphere to which I trespassed, I felt positively welcome.

Gifts of the Gods

Long before I became a househusband, I puzzled over why it was that the higher spiritual qualities—the beatitudes taught by Jesus for example—tended to sound like feminine traits; and why our coarser values, like arrogance or aggressiveness, tended to sound masculine.

Could it be, I now wonder, that the life traditionally offered a woman in our society was, despite the screaming kids, more contemplative than the life of a man? And did this condition make her more open than the rest of us to the higher gifts of the gods?

In my case, even though friends still pray that I will master my sins of arrogance and aggressiveness, I know that my years at home have coincided with a period of more spiritual growth than I was experiencing earlier.

27

Hopefully, these essays reflect some of that.

I believe the women's movement may be helping to right a far deeper inequity than the stated grievances of the women. If a backlash doesn't overtake us too soon, there may be time for the idea of the male role to take a few spiritual strides forward.

The Next Decade?

Looking back on the past seven years, I realize that I have thoroughly enjoyed being a househusband. The ups have far exceeded the downs. Before this, I also enjoyed a career out of the home, and I am richer for having had both experiences.

When I was still a breadwinner, I was beginning to get the feeling of being trapped in a role that I would have to sustain whether I continued to like it or not. I meet many middle-aged contemporaries with the same fear. And we all meet housewives who feel trapped at home. It seems that the frustrations stem not so much from the content of the roles themselves as from the sense of being bound to them. When we are able to move in and out of the breadwinning and homemaking roles, I think that each of them can become a more enjoyable way to live.

Do I now worry about being trapped as a househusband? Not really, though I sometimes like to breast-smite about it. The male career stereotype is every bit as insidious as the homemaking stereotype. After you've escaped one trap, the next one looks nowhere near as threatening.

And what happens after "her decade"? We have no

plans yet. Some of our friends have found ways to work two part-time jobs or to share a job, and these options have appealed to us. We also want to live more of our lives overseas, in societies that are not as highly developed technologically as ours. And once we've paid off some of our horrendous land costs, we may be ready to do a little more toward simplifying our style of living here than the toe-wetting we've done so far. If that goes far enough, we may both quit.

This is a special time in Western culture, when we can explore adaptations to our traditional roles, and do so right in the mainstream of our society. I do not recommend our particular adaptation over other solutions. But I feel that those of us who have stumbled onto fairly workable ways of arranging our lives, can do something useful by sharing what we have found.

At times it can look as if many of us have very little choice as to what roles we can play in life. But at other times we sense that the restrictions around us, if tested, will dissolve.

2

It's a New Day

A few decades ago the hills around here were full of raspberries—and Hopkins, Minnesota was the raspberry capital of the world. Those are rich memories now. The families of Czech homesteaders, whose skill in labor-intensive farming was a legend, have mostly sold out. Some of the more stubborn ones still work a few rows. And a few newcomers like myself have been learning from the old people.

The lessons have ranged beyond raspberry culture.

The first day I took a flat of raspberries to market I expended more emotional energy than I had ever done in a job interview. The scene may have looked unexceptional enough. The produce manager simply grunted at the nervous-looking new vendor and scrawled out a warehouse receipt for twelve dollars. But I had fretted for days over whether I could ever be taken seriously as a primary producer, a doer of meaningful work in the basic capacity of growing food.

Like most of us in our society, I had usually worked as a part of that elaborate structure that "supports" our primary producers. But standing there with my berries, the comfortable rationalizations of that work model were of no help to me. Neither a sales talk on raspberries nor a position paper on hunger would have had any bearing on whether my produce would sell. I was testing a more basic worth, and testing it cold, in a free market.

I drove home in a state of euphoria, and that night Karen had to join me in looking—and looking—at that silly receipt.

A Different Dollar

Raspberries do funny things to economics. They are one of the more expensive items you can buy in the supermarket. Yet I don't know a raspberry farmer who makes a minimum wage picking them, or even a middleman who gets rich on them. Still, raspberry lovers abound, and the growers hate to quit.

One way to explain this is to call it a different dollar. I simply don't compare a dollar earned on the farm with money earned in other pursuits.

"That's fine and dandy," I say to myself one morning in the patch, "but you've got a wife working to make the mortgage payment. You're just playing at farming."

So I concede that.

But I'm still left with questions. Why do I take such pride in those dollars? Why do I sense in so many of my friends a wish that they were out here taming brambles and picking berries in the hot sun?

The answer is not that it's romantic, as some of my city friends think, to work your way hour upon hour through a raspberry patch. Nor is it just a matter of simple rural living. There are lots of rural types whose lives are just as cluttered as those of their city cousins. And there are urbanites whose harmony with their environment is as close as that of any peasant with his.

Simplicity

The explanation may lie in the difference we feel between meeting our basic needs, like food and shelter—and meeting our secondary needs, like the consumer paraphernalia that entraps most of us.

We seem to be in the process, in more advanced technological societies, of learning that the satisfaction we can gain from meeting our basic needs is greater than what we can gain from elaborating on our secondary ones. As a result, we have this longing for whatever looks like a return to simple old-fashioned ways.

Take the wood stove.

I struggle to heat most of our house with wood. Now don't let anyone tell you that it's easier to keep a wood stove going all winter than it is to work an extra ten hours a month for the heating bill. And don't assume there's any defect in my lazy streak; it is wide and healthy. Yet I nurse my stove by choice, and I enjoy it. I suspect a big reason for this is that the stove involves me directly in meeting a basic need of our family.

But one man's satisfaction can be another man's madness. My neighbor sees me in harness, leaning out of the woods with a toboggan load of firewood behind me, and wonders what has possessed me. That compares to my reaction when I see him in summer leaning on a fast rope behind his boat on the lake. I prefer my basic lawn-chair on shore. We are learning to respect each other.

Is It Voluntary?

There is a world of difference between a decision to simplify that is seen as voluntary, and one that is seen as being necessary. Our necessities—personal ones and global ones—can be enormous. At times they can seem overwhelming, so that all the talk about choices is like a bad joke. On behalf of a hungry person or an endangered world, we can argue stridently that it would do most of us good to get along with less. No doubt true. But a more useful service—to ourselves, to our neighbor and to our planet—might be to live the realization that life with less can be a finer life. It can be the life to choose.

That realization has caused people in the main-stream of our society to look for voluntary ways to simplify their lives.

Our choices, happily, need not all be the same. Some choose to live nearer the subsistence level; others look for ways to simplify more affluent living styles. And some of us can be quite inconsistent in deciding when to pick raspberries at a loss, or write essays for profit.

In our ordinary moments, unfortunately, most of us do not think in terms of grandiose choices as to how we will live. More likely, we hang on to some "sweat-of-thy-brow" rationalization for whatever seems to be our lot in life. And that can be grim. In my case, it was not until I had burnt some bridges behind me that I began to see how many options I had before me.

What a Mother-in-law

My mother-in-law stands a generation ahead of most of us in selecting a satisfying life style. In the mid-thirties she and her husband sold a successful trucking business so they could move back to the land. She and her son still earn their livelihood on the family farm in southern Minnesota. Among those who know them, they are generally thought of as having about as good a life as any of us has seen.

But it is a small old-fashioned farm. According to demographers, who have been charting these things since FDR, that family has rarely in all those decades surfaced above the poverty level. Yet their house was full of fun and books, and all the five children have graduate education and are doing their thing from doctoring kids to tinkering with tractors.

In our own family there is no correlation between our affluence curve and our happiness curve. We presently think of ourselves as living fairly affluently, but we attribute a fair amount of our happiness to our decision to live on one full-time income rather than two. And when I look back on my teenage years of going hungry in prison camp, I realize that those memories are not at the top of my list of life's unwanted experiences.

My sister and her husband have upstaged our one income method. They have chosen to live on three-quarters of one income—and it's a modest preacher's income at that. We've never seen them happier.

It does seem harder than it was to put conviction into the snicker with which I used to intone the words, "money isn't everything." There is too much of a grand mixture around us of happy poor, happy rich, sad poor, sad rich—and all the shades in between. Many of us have experienced a variety of these states in our own lives.

The Lao Example

Overseas, the grand mixture takes on bigger proportions. In many countries there are levels both of all-pervasive scarcity and of intense concentration of wealth that far exceed the norms in Western countries. But even at extreme levels of scarcity and affluence, the mixture of happy people and sad ones continues to exist.

When Karen and I worked in Laos in the mid-sixties, our circle of friends belonged to both the ruling elite and to peasant families who had little or no money and grew or bartered for what little they needed. Many of the latter seemed to be happier than I was, churning the dusty streets in my chauffeured sedan.

The Lao are a relaxed and beautiful people. There is a story from that period of an American farm advisor who helped a group of villagers to increase their rice production. At the end of his assignment, the villagers honored him with a feast.

"You have shown us how to double our rice production," they said, "so now we need to plant only half as much rice."

Imagine the exasperation that such a mentality caused in the earnest Western community that was trying to achieve whatever it was we were trying to achieve in Laos. But with the exasperation there was a touch of admiration. And that touch grew on us. In the final analysis, the Lao may have done us more good than we did them, despite our herculean efforts.

Several years later, when Karen and I were weighing a decision to leave the foreign service and try to simplify our lives, we realized that we might never have arrived at that juncture were it not for the example of the Lao.

It's a New Day

A few decades ago, it was not uncommon for one in the U.S. foreign service to prefer a "hardship" assignment in a developing country to being sent "dancing under the chandeliers" in a Western capital. The rationale was that patterns in the old democracies were well established and not likely to change much. The challenge for our generation seemed to be in the Third World, where many options were still open and patterns were being formed that might last for centuries.

Many mistakes later the challenge has shifted.

Now we wish that developing countries would pause a while on their dreary road to modernization. And that our American Congress would recess for a year or two of contemplation. We need a little time now to rethink some basic Western assumptions about the pursuit of happiness in our world.

Fortunately, we Americans have ended our late-lamented decade of anger and confusion. And from surviving that, we have gained an optimism about our society and a sense of mastery over its directions.

Now we need patience. We are doing some serious work, even in raspberry patches. The scale of changes could range from a modest tilt toward simpler life-styles—to a clear shift away from the external and toward the internal aspects of our culture; maybe even to a world consensus on a more advanced perception of reality.

It's a new day.

3
Save the Potato Water

A sally into home economics at this point may be risky, both with those who know the territory better than I do, and with those who may be embarrassed to encounter recipes between the same covers with commentary on the state of our society. Nevertheless:

Having now worked both circuits, I can confirm that

Parkinson's Law prevails in the home as well as in the office.

When time permits, a simple policy decision can plunge a bureaucracy into weeks of earnest position papers, task forces and strategy meetings.

When time permits, a nice little dinner party can plunge the homemaker into weeks of frenzied planning and preparation.

Potato Water

What may be the ultimate reward for a late-blooming househusband occurred to me recently. The woman's editor of our metropolitan paper called to ask about my favorite recipes.

I told her about the potato water.

My mother had taught us to save the water whenever we boiled potatoes. Potato water is handiest as tomorrow's soup. Simply scrape all left-over vegetables, gravy, etcetera into the blender—add your potato water and flip the switch. In a few seconds you will be rewarded with a superb soup.

The name you give this concoction is highly flexible. In the summertime I add a little milk or cream and call it cold vichyssoise. In the wintertime you can throw in a leftover half hamburger and some soy sauce and then serve it piping hot as oxtail soup. Or toss in a teaspoon of curry powder, and you have an exotic curry soup.

My only embarrassment with this dish has been when guests get carried away and ask for the recipe.

Potato water is also the perfect ingredient, along with burnt flour and pan fat, for making a brown gravy that will wean you from those store-boughten supplements.

Pour off all but a few tablespoons of the pan fat. Add enough flour to make a paste. Turn the heat up briefly until the paste turns brown. As you near this point, banish onlookers to the other end of the kitchen, reach for the potato water and—with a Gallic twist of the wrist—douse the works under a dramatic head of steam. Voila! A superb gravy.

Stir-Fry Convenience

Our favorite convenience food was developed in China—stir-fry cooking. Because it also happens to be a superb cuisine, some people reserve it for elaborate occasions. Actually, it's faster than opening and heating a can of spaghetti. And the kids love it. (Don't buy a wok unless you are a purist and have money to waste. A better investment might be an automatic rice cooker.)

Here's a stir-fried convenience. Grab a vegetable or two from the refrigerator. Almost any kind will do: a piece of broccoli, an onion, a green pepper or a small zucchini. While you slice these thin, start the frying pan heating a few tablespoons of oil to hot.

Throw in whatever you've chopped, and stir-fry. Between stirs, mix a small batch of corn starch, soy sauce and a little water. If you want to hide the fact that you forgot to thaw any meat today, add a little chicken bouillon to the mixture. If you feel like being fancy add a little ginger, fresh or powdered. Mix it all together and stir it into the vegetables. Your creation is now ready. The whole process can take less than five minutes.

If you had plugged in an automatic rice cooker a half

hour earlier, you could serve your concoction on steamed rice. You can also eat it straight, or offer it as a sublime vegetable dish with almost any Western fare.

If you want meat in this convenience food, just slice it into thin strips and marinate it for a while in a soy sauce and corn starch mix. Then, stir-fry this mixture for a few minutes and add the vegetables. Superb!

A Touch of Hamburger

Our main meal tends to run heavy on vegetables and light on meat. Even in the winter, when we have fewer home-grown vegetables, we serve either potatoes or rice—plus at least one cooked and one raw vegetable. I rarely use more than a pound of meat to feed our family of six.

Hamburger expands endlessly by adding an egg, a grated onion, some oatmeal or bran—or that half dish of left-over breakfast cereal you made one of the kids save in the refrigerator until after school, but which was never eaten.

To make party fare out of hamburger, I add some pork sausage to my mix, shape my hamburgers a little smaller and a little rounder, whip up a brown gravy (see above), add a pinch of nutmeg, and call the result Norwegian meatballs. (If you are not of Norwegian ancestry, it is more customary to call them Swedish meatballs.)

Serve them with boiled potatoes, buttered carrots, creamed cabbage, and thinly sliced cucumbers sprinkled with sugar, salt and vinegar. It's any easy and elegant way to be a supportive spouse when your wife comes home with business guests.

We rarely get around to dessert at our house. That's mostly because daddy isn't interested and doesn't know much about making them. This may be one reason why all six of us are fairly lean. Another reason may be that our diet has a lot of fiber, so we can be hearty eaters without overloading our systems with calories. My principal objection to restaurant meals, or to party fare, is that everything is too rich.

At breakfast I've given up on getting four kids to share my zest for oatmeal. But I make an optional pot every morning, and most of them eat at least a small portion. We limit ourselves to the sugarless formulations of dry cereals. Sugar is added at the table, self-consciously, with a sly glance to see if parents are watching. We're still 'way ahead of the unconscious sugar sops.

Whenever there is processed snack food in the house it gets eaten, so we try to be fresh out as often as possible. After-school snacks include fruit, crackers, nuts and on ravenous occasions a peanutbutter and jelly sandwich, or two. In theory, I limit snacks so the kids will eat their supper. In practice both institutions thrive. We have soda pop in the house only on special occasions, such as a birthday party.

Shopping for Food

We've gone round and round on what's the best way to shop for food. The neighborhood supermarket is hard to beat for convenience and price. But it is not an uplifting experience to shop there. To begin with, the selection is very blah.

A more serious disadvantage to the chain supermarket stems, I think, from the current fashion in merchandising circles of regarding the customer as a blathering idiot who will clip coupons, paste stamps, or purchase his chinaware by way of buying onions. I have played these games off and on, but I have always felt I was selling my soul for a mess of pottage, and I resented that.

The smaller stores—and the butcher and the greengrocer—are much more civilized; but alas they are often much more expensive as well. The co-ops are cheaper, but they are inconvenient to find and even more inconvenient to shop. I was always afraid I'd lose a child down one of those garbage cans.

We've stumbled onto an agreeable possibility in an unlikely place—a local supermarket that caters to the carriage trade. We started looking at them, after they started buying our raspberries.

Because they sell so many outlandish cuts of expensive meat, they have piles of scrap to feed the hamburger grinder. Excellent ground beef has ranged well below the going price per pound over the past few years.

Similarly, because they carry such an extensive produce selection, they have a table decked with drastically reduced items euphemistically labeled "fully ripe." Here twenty-nine cents will buy you a nice head of lettuce, or a succulent ripe persimmon that was selling for eighty-nine cents the day before. (Anyone who has ever touched his lips to a persimmon that wasn't "fully ripe" will appreciate the irony of this pricing structure.)

If I do most of my shopping on the outer rim of this store, limit myself on imported cheeses, and steer clear of the highly processed items like frozen foods, I can usually match the cost of patronizing a run-of-the-mill supermarket.

In the process, I can feel more civilized, shop from a wide selection, and avoid the more belittling of customary merchandising gimmicks. Finally, there is a wry satisfaction— as I leave the produce and meat counters—in having profited from the folly of conspicuous overconsumers in my society.

From time to time I visit one of the big chains or a co-op to stock up on house brands and bulk items. My impression is that our family eats well and at less cost than some of the other families with whom I have compared notes.

Housecleaning

Friday has been my designated housecleaning day. I confess that my bio-rhythms have responded by making that the day on which I am most likely to yield to a cold or rise to some fervent creative task that cannot possibly be delayed. We can spend Saturday or Sunday catching up, and then Karen will help.

But no Friday has been grim enough to make me consider getting outside help on housecleaning. That would just mean spending Thursday picking up and camouflaging the place from the stranger who would spend Friday invading my privacy. It is one thing to welcome a guest into your living room; but to let someone spend a day poking around in your closets and kitchen cabinets is not to my taste. We had enough of that when we lived overseas with domestic staff.

Four children—with a father who himself never learned much about neatness—can make a horrendous mess of a house. We have always involved our kids in the housework, doing their own rooms and also helping with the common areas. For years this was more trouble than it was worth.

Now it is becoming a marvelous luxury to delegate meaningful hunks of the housework to the capable, if not enthusiastic, hands of the other mess-makers. Our system has been to pay for services rendered rather than to give allowances. During the school year their assignments are fairly light, but in the summertime our kids have the opportunity to earn a nice cash reserve for winter skiing, or to pay for field trips at school.

I suspect most of us keep our homes cleaner than we need to. Earlier generations were not as fastidious as we are. Nor are present Europeans or people in other cultures. I hope we are relaxing a bit.

At our house the big wood furnace in the middle of the living room helps set a less sterilized tone—the chips and splinters around it blend gradually into the thin layer of dust on the coffee table that I hope no one has noticed.

A confession: If one of our male neighbors drops by, it never seems important to clear the cups off the kitchen table. But if it is one of the ladies, I find myself unconsciously doing a fast neatening job. I seem to be drawn into the same cultural mold that draws them, and I need to prove to them that a man can be as conscientious about all this as they can.

Somehow the role changing in our family never filtered down to the laundry room. Whenever I tried taking over, there just seemed to be more colors that ran and fabrics that shrank than my obsessive-compulsive wife could accept. So she never gave up that domain. Over the years we have sparred about the extent to which my incompetence was real or a subconscious manipulation, or even a conscious one. Judgment day will tell.

Recently, our oldest daughter graduated to taking over the laundry from mama—for pay. She started off being both her mother's daughter and her father's little girl. But I think she is turning out to be a lot more like her mother.

Budgets

Household budgets work just like their counterparts in my old jobs. And housepersons can be as irresponsible as bureaucrats. A few ideas that have helped us may be worth considering:

We divide our spending into categories according to how long they do us any economic good. At one end is the eat-drink-and-be-merry variety, whose memories have no economic value the next day. At the other extreme are things like land or housing that tend to be worth more with time. In between are things like cars and books and clothes that expend their usefulness over varying periods of time.

In deciding which expenditures will give us the most pleasure, we try to give a lot of weight to the time factor. This exercise has led us to spending heavily on land and housing. But we buy used cars and run them to the ground, and we hardly ever eat out. We think we get more of the good life for our money this way.

In thinking about wealth, we try to consider the *feeling* that it might produce. For instance, a child feels wealthy with a dollar in her fist. But a surgeon friend of ours is not so lucky. He told us he was starting to enjoy life more now, after having concluded that financial independence was not something that could be achieved—not in a single generation anyway. If there is a discernible pattern here, it is that wealth comes not from any amount of money, but from a feeling that there is more of it than we need.

It follows that if we can design for ourselves a life style that is by choice less elaborate or expensive than our resources permit, we will have the feeling that there is more than we need—the feeling of wealth. Theoretically, at least, the feeling of wealth is available at any standard of living.

4
Look At Mama-Duck

At this writing the kids are 10, 11, 12 and 13 years old—bursting into their teens.

And they still don't pick up their socks.

It is hardly a prudent time to write an essay on parenting. It might be wiser to ask parents who have run the full course for their urgent advice on how to reach the finish line. But I have now had seven years of experience as the primary parent in a large family, and can share some mid-course observations.

There She Waddles

I see them now from the window. The chances of mama duck succeeding in raising her brood seem even more remote than mine. In the woods around her are fox and raccoon. And prowling the yard is Bruno, the dog. All of them are eager, at odd moments, to devour her offspring. In fact, she got a late start this year because Bruno ate her first batch of eggs.

Besides, she's never had a course in parenting. Yet she figured out how to make a nest and how to achieve the total concentration of her energies that let her sit for four weeks incubating her eggs.

I had my come-uppance over that incubation period. I was sure she had sat much too long, so I called the Agricultural Extension Service and got through to the old poultry professor. He assured me the incubation period was 28 days. Then he decimated me:

"My suggestion to you would be this: If she has not lost patience, Sir, neither should you."

The next day she began hatching.

And there she waddles, proceeding so naturally to introduce her young to the world of healthy, coping, adult ducks. Since she seems to do it so effortlessly, it puzzles me that I should have to think of parenting as one of the hardest jobs I have had in my life. I have no reason to believe that the human instinct for parenting is any weaker than the anatine one, or the male of our species any less equipped for parenting than the female. I note that my sister colleagues seem to court a sense of near disaster as parents just about as frequently as I do.

Of course, if mama duck could intellectualize about parenting the way people do, she might sound just as overwhelmed by it all.

She would insist that Bruno is more lethal than any drug pusher at school.

She would nod knowingly as I explain how utterly exhausted I can be after marshalling four sets of coats, snowboots, gloves (preferably matched) and hats—each with a child inside, and all in time to catch the school bus. That's nothing, she might say, compared to the maddening frustration of trying to steer her brood from the pond to the barn.

She saves us this chatter. Instead, she acts out an ideal of parenting that is common to both our species. I have found it useful as a parent to sit and think about how well mama-duck does my job.

"Superstimulus"

Why, for example, do I become so readily consumed with running my kids from sewing lessons to swimming lessons to French lessons? Why do I feel so obliged to immerse myself in all those school activities that come under the umbrella of "enrichment"?

In the zest for planned activity that characterizes our society, it is useful to have mama-duck around to remind us that much of what we call parenting is "superstimulus." We would probably do a better job as parents if we could set a simple example in a nurturing environment, and then allow our kids to learn for themselves without too much interference.

51

Whole Parents

Mama-duck does not separate parenting from the rest of survival. In the normal course of things her offspring are exposed to the whole design of how a duck lives. This is true of parenting in most species and in most human societies. Ours is an exception, and it may explain why we have to work so hard at being good parents.

I remember the scene when a part of this manuscript was being reviewed by a local publisher. This successful house was very much a "mom and pop" operation; their kids were running in and out of the editorial conference. At one point our discussion halted so the youngest could do her "show and tell" from nursery school. I liked it. I think many of us wish we could recreate the "old days" when parents and children and extended families worked and played together on farms and in towns. There are some moves in this direction, but it is not easy.

We are a society of specialists, and most of us are expert in only a few aspects of our lives. Parenting, like everything else, has tended to become a neat little specialty of its own. And for several generations now, breadwinning—a central part of our lives—has been isolated from the rest of family life.

There are signs of a corrective phase. More of us want to be generalists. More of us are inclined to find ways of sharing the roles of parenting and breadwinning. This tends to improve our lives as adults. And by taking turns at parenting, we hope to expose our children to broader role models.

But even this is less than whole parenting. In our

family the kids will assure you that they now see more than enough of their dad. But mama works sixty or seventy hours per week, much of it away from home. Fortunately, she can involve the kids in some of her work, and she is very good at being close to her children, even at the end of a hard day.

Still, mama-duck reminds us that we should keep looking in our culture for a more workable way to integrate parenting with the whole fabric of our lives.

Learning to Cope

The farming in our family is a stab at recreating the old days when parents and children had similar agendas. We try to involve the whole family in the housework and the farming. This causes some static at times, but we believe it is one of the healthier family activities we have found. It sure beats TV.

It can even be a riotous comedy—as on the day our kids were selling apples at the top of the driveway. A jogger panted up and asked the price of one apple. Twenty-five cents, said a fast-thinking child—and added, after a first delicious bite, that the gentleman might be able to carry two. It then developed that no one had change for a dollar. The jogger was last seen limping over the hill, still trying to tuck four apples into sundry parts of his sweating anatomy.

Last Christmas the kids overwhelmed us with spontaneous home-made gift certificates. One promised to carry half a cord of wood up to the porch, two of them promised a week's worth of washing dishes, and one offered two weeks of snow shoveling.

Despite such occasional reassurances, however, there remains an important respect in which this arrangement is a contrived one. The kids know and we know that their contribution to the work at home is not crucial to the well-being of our family. I think this is a very serious drawback to growing up in an affluent society.

Karen and I had childhoods that would be thought of as stressful by today's criteria—she with her cows and I in the prison camp. We both look back on such experiences as positive ones that helped us grow rather than limit us. We have not had the courage to wish for similar stresses on our own children, but we wonder whether we are not holding them back by our lack of courage.

It does not at all surprise me that some of the nicest and most competent children in that circle of friends our kids bring home come from families that are stressed in some way—as for instance a single parent family where the boy has to babysit and sometimes cook for his sister while Mother is working. If the experts would classify him as a high-risk child, I think they are way off the mark.

Values

When the kids were younger, we once had to drag them out of an Easter Sunrise Service at Wolftrap Farm outside Washington because the religious pantomime being presented was as loaded with gratuitous violence as a grade B movie.

One enormous advantage that mama-duck has over the rest of us is that she is indisputably the dominant influence over her brood during the formative period. Her values are consistent and unquestionable. In our society we start with a plurality of values, even within families, and then we discover that we are sharing the modeling stage with a whole cast of monuments to ambivalence.

Two of the more overwhelming of these must be television and school.

Fortunately ambivalence is a paper tiger. So long as any of us possesses a set of personal values, even if we are no more than trying to live up to them, it can be ammunition enough to confront the ambivalence around us. Not that our values will become those of our children. But it is important to offer them a stable value base from which to build their own.

Television

Our TV set is a study in downplay—a battered black-and-white portable with a metal coat hanger poking out where the rabbit ears used to be. It works.

The usual rule has been to limit TV-watching to one hour per day, with parental rights to veto selections we consider too violent, or too sexy, or too just plain dumb. Last year, when the kids started having more homework, we tried to eliminate weekday watching in favor of more time on weekends. This worked fairly well—but there seem to have been endless specials for which exceptions had to be considered.

If our kids sometimes think they are missing out, and if they gawk at neighboring color consoles, these are lesser evils, we think, than what we believe they are escaping.

Schools

We have not found a neat solution to the problem of schools. This is sobering, since our family has already accumulated 38 child-years of experience with schools—eight in nursery schools, 28 years with suburban public schools in Virginia and Minnesota, and two years of private school experience. They have been years of earnest parental involvement, from room "mothering," to volunteering for countless enrichment schemes, to leadership in numerous parent-teacher groups.

Last year we moved two of our four children from public school into a small evangelical Christian school. We hope the church school might do more than the public school to help our children build some basic tools of thought—such as a value base and skills with the language and with numbers.

There were some surprises in comparing the two systems.

The Christian school, operating on a shoestring budget and with a minimum physical plant, seemed to be running circles around our big fat public school system in terms of academic achievement.

But in the value corner, the results were mixed.

The Christian schools, whose teachings we understood and respected from our backgrounds, did reinforce many of our family values, especially in its emphasis on both a personal accountability and an access to grace.

But we found that the church school kids were much more tuned in to material things like big cars and family affluence than were their public school peers. Our daughter, who at public school had never given a thought to the condition of her jeans, became clothes-conscious almost overnight. We had to re-emphasize that eloquent advice of Jesus to "consider the lil-lies. . . ."

We were pleased to find our public school scoring rel-atively high as a source of positive values, especially in comparison with a school that thought it had a corner on this sport.

But there remains a fundamental problem with value teaching in our public schools. It stems from the fact that we are a society embracing a plurality of values. And the dominant theme of our secular value system is still what E. F. Schumacher called "a view of the world as a wasteland in which there is no meaning or purpose, in which man's consciousness is an unfortunate cosmic accident, in which anguish and despair are the only final realities."*

Granted, there are some lovely new currents of mean-ing stirring in our land.

But for the present it is unlikely that our public schools can achieve much more or less than ambivalence in trying to expose our children to a value structure. This essential element of an education has to come from else-where, preferably from the family.

Our local school system currently offers a pathetic il-lustration of this point. It is embarked on a program to teach all fourth graders about drug abuse before their peers misdirect them. We had to pull our fourth grader out of the program because it lacked a clear position on

---

*E. F. Schumacher, *Small Is Beautiful*, Harper & Row; 1975, p. 84.

what was good or bad about drugs, and there was no way of predicting whether the instruction would increase or decrease the likelihood of a child turning to drugs. Yet the intentions of the educators seemed earnest indeed.

As parents, I think the wisest thing we can do is to steer our public schools away from perpetuating a mishmash of diluted values, and to give our children whatever we can of our own values to build on.

If our society should arrive at a new consensus on better ways to live and think, we can then consider letting our schools back into the value business. (We might even let them pray again.)

The Scarlet Letter

We can be as heartless in our labelling as any previous century. The term "at risk" pinned on a child by a teacher or counselor can be as devastating to a life as was the scarlet "A." The problem is not one of people wanting to be heartless. It is one of their needing the assurance of simplistic categories in fields where few absolutes exist.

From 'round the clock exposure to our four children—two biological and two adopted—I know that all of them, like their father, are operating at a tiny fraction of the level of their innate and learned capacities. Our peers recognize this, and seem to honor all of us with an equal irreverence. The problem comes with the professionals.

In my experience, the single most difficult aspect of being an adoptive parent has been that of finding ways to whisk off the "at risk" labels being pinned on my kids by professionals who ought to know better.

At our school this madness reached a level where the counselor would try to assemble all single-parent kids, adopted kids, and sundry other "at risk" categories into a regular group counselling session—away from those other kids labeled "normal"—where they could share each others' feelings of inadequacy—and reinforce them.

My wife reports that she and her colleagues are seeing an increasing number of children who have been labelled and placed into group counseling sessions at school, without their parents' knowledge or consent. Some are declared "over aggressive," others are labelled "too shy," and some are tossed into that wide bin marked "learning disabled," which seems to have included some extraordinarily gifted children—even Albert Einstein.

Any child can confirm an "at risk" category, or be among the exceptions to that data base. It is as logical to think of a child one way as the other. But one of these expectations is incarcerating, the other is liberating. The story of Pygmalion is as valid as ever.

If you have trouble with this argument, find a raspberry patch. My pickers have ranged from learned academicians to kids plastered with bad labels. Through the hot afternoon, we all do some nibbling, we all pick about the same number of pints, and when we arrive at the end of the rows we all feel relieved of some of the heavier of our labels.

Expectation

There is a final lesson from mama-duck. It is her

deepest secret of parenting and a deceptively simple one.

She operates on the utterly unshakable assumption that she is fully equipped for whatever the task of parenting will require. When we stop to think about it we realize that this inner assurance pervades all nature. How else, in fact, do we humans manage to cut through all the cognitive baggage of our civilization and manage to raise young ones who can function in as complicated a society as ours?

We may ponder why it is that so many of us can be so unaware so much of the time that we are genetically so well equipped for whatever the task of parenting will require. This gap in our awareness is no esoteric threat to parenting. Rather, in a houseful of kids, the inner secret that we can expect to be good parents is one of the best things we can have going for us.

When we fail as parents, it is easy in our specialized society to blame it on poor technique or on having encountered the wrong role models. I think it is more accurate, at a deeper level, to conclude that we had an inadequate expectation of ourselves as good parents.

This does not diminish the importance to all of us, including mama-duck, of our role models and learning experiences as parents. But it is good to remind ourselves that we arrived in the world magnificently endowed to be good parents. To argue otherwise we would have to insist that we are the sole exception to the evidence in all of life around us that the surviving species are very good at perpetuating themselves.

The Powerful Present

There is a very reassuring lesson we can draw from all this:

If indeed we can be taught to forget our instinct to be good parents, it follows that we can also be taught to reawaken that instinct. Furthermore, if inadequate role models and experiences in the past can make us poor parents today, it follows that good models and good experiences today can make us better parents tomorrow.

Ever since freshman psychology, I have puzzled over that hoary argument about whether it is our heredity or our environment that has made us what we are.

I now believe that both sides missed the point. The human animal does not need to be dominated either by his heredity or his environment, unless he and his society decide in the present to accept the domination of one or the other, or both. The point of power for us is always the present. We can redirect ourselves and our expectations of each other whenever we are sufficiently motivated to do so.

In the thick of parenting, unfortunately, we rarely have time to think very broadly about what we are doing. Our focus tends to be on solving the immediate problem, whether it's wet beds or unacceptable backtalk or something else.

We are attracted by clear and simple "methods" that promise to remove the specific problem. But most of us have failed at more methods than we care to remember. And we have also succeeded at odd moments when it seemed we weren't doing anything, right or wrong, to trigger that success. I recall years of failure at trying to teach my son not to lose his gloves. But I have no clear recollection of how the problem went away, other than a strong suspicion that it occurred shortly after I quit trying and stopped worrying about it.

Changing Expectations

From a mid-course perspective as a primary parent, I believe the most useful lesson I can pass along is that my outcomes seem to be responding to my expectations rather than to my methods.

I must also confirm that it can sometimes seem quite impossible, in the thick of things, to achieve any consistency in living with positive expectations. But on the occasions when I do lock in on a vivid image of a desired outcome, I am reassured by the ensuing harvest of happy coincidences.

In trying to erase my negative expectations and substitute positive ones, I have found it useful to start by quieting my physical body, usually through one of the relaxation techniques that are widely taught. Once the body is quiet, it becomes easier to still the mind, and to allow negative impressions to dissipate. I aim for as clean a mental screen as possible, on which I can let form a desired new set of feelings, images and expectations.

Forcing this process never seems to work. If I cannot effortlessly imagine that my daughter will pick up her room this week without my nagging, I gently amend the image to what I can achieve without effort, maybe visualizing her next spring routinely picking up her room.

I have found it helpful to be able to integrate this process with my religious heritage, and I have learned from people of different religious backgrounds that the same is true in their case. For Christians the process is easily understood as prayer, about which Jesus taught us, "If you believe, you will receive whatever you ask for in prayer."

In conclusion, I am discovering that the best place to work at being a good parent is inside my own mind. It is there that I must decide whether I will let the nitty gritty of the job determine my expectations of my children—or whether I will deliberately fix in my mind a dominant image of them growing into happy, coping, and contributing adults. I believe enough of us parents will manage to choose the latter approach to surprise both the experts and our beleagured selves.

5

The Good Life

Mercifully, there is more to being a doctor's spouse than the stereotype of mink coats and bridge parties. Like the work roles, our leisure roles are expanding beyond the old norms.

Admittedly, most of us are still imprinted with the notion that the more money we can throw away on our diversions the more fun they will be. But we are slowly learning to improve on that script.

We may also be learning, from our surfeit of TV and other spectator lures, that entertaining ourselves can be more fun than being entertained—a new idea that's as old as our idealized past.

Some of us are learning from the land.

Hobby farming—once a toy of the privileged rich—is now enjoyed by a privileged band that operates on all economic levels— even on the subsistence level. Our own initiation occurred in the early seventies when we borrowed to the limit to settle on 3 1/2 acres outside Washington.

It was a world of hairy excitements that overtook us.

Cattle Grazing

Despite the sensible influence of my farm-girl wife, we ventured into cattle grazing fifteen miles from the White House.

It started innocently with one little steer in our pasture. When a Huguenot neighbor saw that it was a Charolais, he came by to lecture us on its French ancestry. Whereupon the children lapsed into Franglais, naming the critter Fleur de White, and made it their pet.

But by late summer the pet was pawing the grass and making snorting noises. So we asked Ancher Nelsen of Minnesota, a legitimate dirt farmer in Congress, for his advice. He emerged from the barn, sober and splattered, to announce, "It's a bull!"

We sold early that year.

The second year we doubled our herd. This time they both stayed steers, and all went fairly well, except that our meat would have been cheaper at the supermarket.

The third year we were wiped out!

Two skittish Herefords arrived from auction, took one look around our paddock and jumped the fences. (Had the farm girl been home, she would have unloaded them into the barn.)

For three weeks the steers roamed free, broadening their taste for varieties of lawngrass, and varieties of suburban hysteria. We tracked them daily, and sightings were recorded on a chart in the kitchen. But they had learned to jump fences, so there was no catching them. The authorities were as helpless as we were.

In desperation we called Frank Abercrombie at the World Bank. Frank was a New Mexico cowboy who went by the bureaucratic title of "range management consultant." He had been our neighbor in Nairobi, Kenya.

"You git me a quarterhorse," drawled Frank, "and ah'll point those critters raht up your driveway."

We located an aging but serviceable quarterhorse from Montana, now living about a mile from our place. For the next two weekends, horse-crazy Northern Virginia was treated to some superb riding.

But, alas, those fences. They had killed a way of life in the West, and here they were thicker than in any cowboy's nightmare.

On a rainy afternoon the two steers, followed by Frank on the horse, churned their way across one of the largest and stateliest lawns in the county. They came upon the highest and sturdiest fence they had seen. The steers mustered their energy for a final leap. Frank turned to face the lady of the estate. Fortunately, she was a cattle lover; the steers had jumped to join her registered herd.

Soon the vet was there to calm them, and shortly thereafter they were sold—a hundred dollars lighter for their adventure.

I went back to growing vegetables.

Organic Apples?

Then we moved to Minnesota, and suddenly the hobby jumped to near-commercial proportions. Our place had apples, nursery stock, and raspberries. I took crash courses at the Vo-Tech, and had to become more serious about the hobby. But the sense of wonderment remained, as did the occasional sense of near panic.

What, for example, should we do about those 100 beautiful apples trees, ready to drop their first crop? I made the mistake of asking the County Agent how to grow organic apples—and had to endure his laughter. We then made "underground" inquiries and located a successful organic orchard in another state.

There, to our horror, we were told, "If you want to grow good organic apples, you have to do some spraying."

It was not as cynical a remark as it sounded. The theory was that a good apple grower, instead of willy-nilly spraying the works every seven days or so, might better spend his time following the life cycles of all living things in his orchard, and then intervening specifically with pruning or compost or lady bugs or chemical sprays whenever something threatened to get out of hand. In practice, however, this grower's spray schedule seemed not much lighter than that of the big, bad department of agriculture, and the poisons he used were far more toxic than the garden varieties available to hobbyists.

In the end my purist resolve weakened, and we have followed a minimum schedule of the broad spectrum spraying recommended for home growers. Meanwhile, it is a hopeful sign that some professional farmers have started looking beyond high technology for better ways to grow things and better ways to live.

There are people who make money on hobby farming, but so far we are not among them. We barely cover operating costs, not counting my labor or the cost of carrying the land.

But we keep expecting to do better next year. And we still think that the price of living on the land, even expensive land close to urban areas, compares favorably with the cost of the other ways our society offers to escape the urban grind: vacation homes, boats, recreational vehicles, ski vacations, etc.

Fortunately, all of these escapes have their avid supporters. If not, the cost of land would have soared even higher.

Living productively with rural land will, I suspect, shake out as the single most desirable way to live in an advanced technological society.

On the Town

In our experience, once you get hooked on something like land, there is less appeal to some of the traditional diversions of our society, like big nights on the town. This may be sour grapes, since all the extra money goes for land, but I don't think so.

I have a househusband's appreciation for getting out

of the kitchen once in a while to enjoy a prepared meal.

But consider what we are asked to endure in the average restaurant.

There is, first of all, the matter of our tax laws, which in effect permits some of us to eat out in lieu of paying more taxes. As a result, we can eye each other at adjoining tables, feeling either vaguely resentful because we can't deduct the cost of this meal, or vaguely guilty if we can. Both are bad for the digestion.

Then there are the appeals to our inadequacies.

Tipping is an example. Rather than asking the full price of the meal, a part of the price is extracted in the form of an exploitation of our desire to feel more adequate than the person waiting on us. At more expensive restaurants we are permitted to prove our adequacy by tipping a captain as well as a waiter.

If we have a dependency on alcohol or nicotine, we are likely to feel encouraged to drink more and smoke more in a restaurant than we would at home. To decline a cocktail or to try avoiding the smoke tends to fall into the same category with snoring in church.

Even the decor and entertainment we encounter are commonly appeals, subtle or otherwise, to our sexual inadequacies.

We must have these inadequacies, or the system would long since have petered out.

But we also have strengths. Once we sort out our tax laws, there should be a growth market in this affluent society for restaurants and night spots that cater to strengths rather than weaknesses. If a few better restaurants would start offering no-tipping menus, like no-smoking tables, I think the practice would spread rapidly.

At the other end of the eatery business, ironically, the new market has already been discovered. The fast food chains are succeeding, even with their dull fare, partly because they offer a consistent product at a consistent price—with no murky requirements to prove something to yourself or to others.

On the few occasions when we eat out as a family, it tends to be at one of these chains, or at buffets or cafeterias. I suspect there are lots of us around who would occasionally like to live a little higher off the hog than that, and we think restaurants can grow up to tap this market.

As for entertaining among friends, we were scarred in the foreign service from a surfeit of dreary stand-up and sit-down affairs, weighted before, during and after the vittles by an excess of alcohol and small talk. We now enjoy an occasional informal evening with just a few people, or an afternoon picnic that includes the kids.

But honest conversation can bless any gathering, even a large one, or a formal one.

Television

There are signs that the powerful spell television has cast over us for a generation is lifting. For instance, there is a growing minority of us with sketchy views on the subject, because we don't watch enough of it to form an opinion.

I think we have tired of letting the spectator role consume so much of our leisure time.

I also suspect we are tired of contorting ourselves into a mass audience when, in fact, we are a whole array of little audiences with individual interests. The next step may be for TV to abandon the mass audience concept in favor of programming for little audiences.

My guess is that we are in the process of relegating television, like we did radio, into something nice to have around when it suits us, but not central to our lives.

Try getting that across to four kids! Our defensive strategy—described in the last chapter—has been to limit them to one hour a day at the tube.

Ideally, none of us should need to impose our opinions of TV on others. If my wish for the moment is nothing more than to vegetate over one of TV's more banal offerings—or conversely, to give the tube a swift kick—I should be free to do so, and let the critics be damned.

But television does operate on publicly-owned broadcast frequencies, and it does have awesome power to entrap us, and it does tend to use that power to exploit our weaknesses. So the outcry against TV is understandable. But sputtering at the program makers is not as powerful a reform tool as the simple assertion of our individuals strengths at the control buttons on our sets.

Amateur Talent

A visit to a charity bazaar or handicrafts counter in the United States can now be just as rewarding as a stroll through the market place of an agrarian society with a strong tradition in handicrafts. Our output is really becoming very good.

Our adult education departments have grown topsy-turvey to meet the demands of people who have tired of spectator leisure and want to develop their talents for self-fulfillment.

More and more of us would rather clutter our homes

with the modest creations of our friends and ourselves than with the professional output.

If one of us can persuade a passable amateur musician to try out his own compositions on our out-of-tune piano, that is likely to raise more goosepimples than a digital Horowitz.

And on those occasions when others will suffer a show of our own talent, that—if we don't flub too much—can be sheer heaven. Each of us, of course, has his own act. In my case, bliss comes at the piano, improvising the harmony of some Welsh hymn and surrounded by friends belting out a classic like "Guide me, O Thou great Jehovah, Pilgrim through this barren land."

The measure of those friendships is that they all know I can't read music, that I play only by ear, play only hymns, and only in C or in sharps—never in flats.

Do-It-Yourself

The do-it-yourself mystique has penetrated far beyond the home repairs industry that gave it birth. And it is much more than a response to the high cost of services. I think it is becoming an important symbol of the good life in our society.

The best winter of my tenure as househusband so far was the one I spent designing and helping to build an addition to our home. As a student I had started out to be an architect, but became distracted by radio announcing. I ended up choosing to minor in the subject. Ever since then I have dabbled with plans and longed for the day when I might turn a plan into a structure. To have that opportunity was ecstasy.

To grow your own food—and to be able to heap your plate with a cornucopia of your own produce—must be one of life's great luxuries. I relish the memory of the day we had vegetarian guests and were able to offer a spread that included twelve varieties of home-grown vegetables.

It can be an endless list of do-it-yourself ideas: to take tax courses and do my own battles with the revenue agent—to learn from the neighbor how to keep the old "G-Allis" tractor running—to work at building a personal life style and value system—and to be my own publisher when I write a book about it. These are luxuries in life.

The Ultimate Hobby

Each of us will have our own candidate for this label—some activity we see as the quintessence of the good life for ourselves and for others. I offer mine.

The ultimate hobby is to daydream.

If that sounds strange, it is because we are adults in a society that asked us to sacrifice daydreaming in our rites of passage. But a child can still close his eyes and watch his favorite TV show, or take a swim, or build his castle. And now adults are relearning this art.

Daydreaming is the generic component of the "gone fishing" formula. It is also the reason (along with the tan) why we see more people lying on the beach than we see swimming in the water. These were ways in which we camouflaged daydreaming in the days before it became respectable for adults just to daydream.

Now we can lapse into our private world at the drop

of an imaginary eyelid. We think nothing of finding ourselves in no particular place, doing no particular thing, for no particular reason.

What a luxury!

Like many hobbies, daydreaming can be enjoyed casually or intensely.

The casual hobbyist might light upon a pleasant thought and allow his mind to pursue it like a butterfly in a garden.

More serious hobbyists try to control their reverie on the silent hunch that there are no "idle" thoughts and that what they live within they experience without.

Other hobbyists narrow their focus to the contemplation of one thing and gain therefrom a serenity about all things. Some of the greatest daydreamers have had religions named after them. "As a man thinketh in his heart, so is he."

Happy dreams.

Part Two

Exploring Ways to Think

6

The Jericho Principle

When the walls of Jericho fell flat, a magnificently defended city surrendered to aggression from a band of nomads who had become convinced that the city would fall to them after a prescribed sequence of shouting and trumpet blaring.

Millenia later, a superbly equipped superpower

abandoned Indochina to a group of peasants who had become convinced that their ideology was the wave of the future.

When I worked as a journalist in the fifties and a diplomat in the sixties, I gave little thought to Joshua's exploits. My jobs were to explain the present. But in the raspberry patch both those careers seem a little more understandable in the context of what can be called the Jericho Principle.

Laos

I worked for the U.S. Information Agency from 1961 to 1972. During those years the dominant issue in foreign affairs was Southeast Asia. And the dominant feature of that decade was the extent to which it evaded all other influences except people's opinions.

USIA was in the business of opinions, communicating with people of other nations on behalf of our society and government. We made only small dents in world opinion during that decade but, in retrospect, we did learn something about the importance of our stock in trade—opinions.

When I went to Laos in 1961, I reflected my society's uncomplicated conviction that we should help sort out the mess in that area and encourage the growth of a nice community of viable noncommunist nations. We expected that this might serve our national interest, but we were doing it mainly because it had to be done and no one else seemed ready to take the responsibility.

A measure of our confidence was that the USIA program in Laos dropped most of the traditional "telling-

America's-story" aspects of our work. Instead our emphasis was on helping the Lao rebuild their sense of nationhood after a half century of being the boondocks of French Indochina.

The characteristic grace and charm of the Lao people did much to diffuse the conflicts that were swirling around them.

I remember the tense Fourth of July, 1962, in Vientiane. The latest Geneva conference, with U.S. support, had just patched up a tripartite Lao government of rightist, neutralist and communist factions. U.S. military advisors were flown out of the country, and Yankee-hating rebel leaders began coming out of the hills to take their places in the coalition. The neutralist Premier, Prince Souvanna Phouma, was still in Paris. We wondered who, if anyone, would represent the new government at our Fourth of July reception.

The first touch of Lao grace came early in the day. A noisy military convoy descended on the American Embassy bearing, in a universal gesture of humanity, one basket of fresh vegetables—with the compliments of the rightist leader, Prince Boun Oum. And that evening, as spines tingled, the new Communist Vice Premier, Prince Souphanouvong, made his first public appearance to toast the friendship between the people of Laos and the people of the United States.

As it turned out, the coalition itself never worked. But the charm worked throughout the decade, helping insure that the level of confrontation in Laos was always many notches below what it was in neighboring Vietnam.

After our military group had gone, I remember taking

quiet delight that our efforts in Laos were no longer being dominated by what had seemed like the clumsiness of their presence. But coupled with this feeling was one of quiet disdain for the fuzzy notion that a coalition government could end in anything but communist domination.

To my great surprise, the communists pulled out, leaving the field to the neutralist and rightist factions. By the mid-sixties the soul of Lao nationalism was clearly both neutralist and looking to the U.S. to help it survive. There was much irony in this, especially with the mounting noise from our own left, but the point was soon lost in all the confusion over Vietnam itself.

Washington

In the mid-sixties we spent two years in Washington. It was the period of the light at the end of the tunnel. I worked at the Voice of America, heading the Korean Service. VOA was trying to reflect both official government policy and the growing divisions in our society over Southeast Asia and other issues. That we were able to ride this dilemma at all was probably more remarkable than the occasional fracases that erupted.

My favorite VOA story concerns the news item we received one day that Fidel Castro's sister had defected to the West. The translators in many of the 33 languages of VOA insisted that the story was untranslatable unless it was known whether this was the older or the younger sister. Their languages had words for one variety or the other, but no word for sisters in general. In a rich confluence of sibling memories and propaganda zeal we all agreed that, if an arbitrary decision must be made, it would be the older sister.

VOA also reported the frequent weekend anti-war demonstrations around the White House. I was proud that we could do this, but I was unable to accept the protestors' cause.

One Sunday I walked over there and became sufficiently polarized that I decided to counterdemonstrate. Leaving the milling unwashed, I came upon the small neat band of Americans for Freedom. Alas, their slogans were as simplistic as those of their opponents. I could not carry one. Someone gave me an American flag, and I walked briefly with that, but I was ashamed of where my American Dream had taken me. I thought of Rudyard Kipling's "If," and vowed to try harder to stay unpolarized.

Southeast Asia was now the growth industry in Washington. In an epidemic of "funds-are-available" we saw brilliance and boorishness, nobility and selfishness swirling around us and within us as we rushed to develop programs and build careers.

Laos Again

In 1966 I had six months of intensive Lao language training and went back to Laos as deputy director of our information program there. My wife became deputy director of the public health program in the AID mission to Laos.

Back among Lao friends, we began to realize how peripheral their aspirations had become in our great debate about the war. Our rift was an internal identity crisis, having to do with values in our own society.

An outward expression of it took the form of slogans purporting to "end the war" or "resist aggression" in Southeast Asia. But at one pole we could not stop to think how tragically inappropriate our massive technology was for the job in Southeast Asia. And at the other pole we could not stop to think that the people over there really wanted and needed the services of a competent world policeman. At our respective poles, one thought or the other had to be blindly rejected as too threatening.

The Lao had their own contradictions. One morning General Ma, the zealous Lao Air Force commander, dispatched his entire force (several dozen World War II trainers) in battle formation over Vientiane and showered his capital with bombs. His target was the General Staff, whose sins included diverting his planes on gold or opium missions. His unintended victims were hundreds of ordinary citizens.

By reasonable standards for that society, Prince Souvanna Phouma's neutralist government was exceptionally broadly based, having held together all serious factions in the country except the Pathet Lao—the small indigenous Communist movment. But beyond the towns along the Mekong, the government's influence was only sporadic. Large open areas of the country, like the Ho Chi Minh Trail, were controlled by the North Vietnamese.

One of the more remarkable aspects of those years in Laos was the poker game played by our Ambassador William Sullivan—with Premier Souvanna Phouma's support—to contain the incessant pressures from Hanoi and from the Pentagon and Saigon for expanding their operations into Laos. The cost of such a tightly held hand was that many people missed the point. Our biggest public relations problem became the determination of the world press to document "the secret war in Laos."

Before we left Laos in 1968 we had the good fortune to be able to adopt a Lao daughter from the orphanage where Karen had worked during both our tours in the country. It sealed into our family's genealogy the impact made on us by the graceful and long-suffering people of Laos.

Kenya

After Laos it was a nice decompression to be press attache in Nairobi. Here, there were no urgent U.S. foreign policy objectives. We wanted to give a modest boost to Kenya's economic development, but mainly our job was to help sustain the generally friendly detachment with which Kenyans and Americans had tended to see each other.

The space program had caught the imagination of everyone from Richard Leakey to the kids in the shamba.

I remember the week we took one of the first moon rocks on tour to all of Kenya's provinces. Geology students from the University were exhibit guides; the Kenyan police and Kenya Air Force provided transportation and screeching escorts wherever we went; Barclay's bank opened their vaults for overnight storage; and everyone, so it seemed, saw the rock.

Karen capped the week with a classic April Fool's Day trick! The rock was back in the Embassy safe, and I was finally soaking in the tub. I heard the phone, and Karen answering it.

"It's not in the safe? Yes, I'll get him right away."

(Every year she tries to top that one, and she probably will. My efforts to counter fool her are always flops!)

I remember pondering that silly piece of charcoal, wondering how it was that I and everyone else should be so awed by it that we had to treat it like the Hope diamond, and realizing that the proposition was really the other way around: the hoopla had made the value; the effect had created the cause. But I had not yet thought about Jericho.

By this time the turmoil and divisions in our society were fairly accurately reflected in the minds of those of us working on overseas information—and properly so, since that was our job.

We told the Kenyans more than they wanted to know about our troubles in Vietnam. On civil rights, we belabored both the advances of the sixties and how much there was left to do. When congressional investigators swooped in to check our library shelves (in ironic replay of Cohn and Schine), we could point with pride to our neat display of *Soul On Ice*.

The Kenyans kindly ignored us. They had enough of their own troubles. Kenya was everybody's favorite example of a developing country: strong people with a stable government, vigorous economic growth, a magnificent modern capital, and breath-taking game parks.

Almost all the developed countries—and scores of private organizations—had established aid programs in Kenya. ("Why didn't I see you in Laos," I would tease my Scandinavian friends.)

But for all the superb effort, something seemed to be wrong. Rich traditional life styles (the Masai for a dramatic example) were giving way to crowds of unemployed on the streets of Nairobi. Almost daily we were turning away determined young graduates wanting jobs as writers (or anything) and we tried to do it without fraying their noble dream of "Harambee" (pull together).

If this was the best example of an emerging new nation, then maybe we needed to re-examine some Western materialistic assumptions about the blessings of becoming modern.

Jericho

Washington in the early seventies was an awesome seat from which to feel the crumbling of our national self-confidence and self-control.

I remember that May Day when the anti-war movement set out to close the place down. My bus made it to the Theodore Roosevelt Bridge. In the four hours it took to walk the last mile to work, I sustained a fervent rap with any activist who would talk. Regrettably, I did not understand a one of them, and none of them understood me.

Years later I began realizing how tantalizingly close some of us had been to saying the same thing, only from different perspectives. They were angry and disillusioned, while for me that first generation armor had somehow held around my American dream.

I was glad to be able to leave the government in 1972

and to tune out the media. The private dream survived
in the househusband. Eventually we all began meeting
others with quiet dreams that grew and mixed until we
could say that it was again a common dream and that
our society had survived.

And we became strong enough to wonder, "What
happened?"

A Nation's Power

The Jericho Principle asserts that the outcome of our
conflicts are determined by the prevailing expectations
in a case rather than by its merits or the external power
factors involved in it.

Merit and power can be important in shaping a prevailing expectation. But if they do not accomplish this,
they will not by themselves determine an outcome.

In our clearer moments, most of us have recognized
that variations on this principle seem to operate in all
human affairs. For many of us, though, it is hard to ap-
ply this wisdom with much consistency in the way we
run our lives. It is even more rare to find it applied to the
affairs of a society. The result is much confusion over the
eccentric outcomes of public policy.

Take, for example, our defense budgets over the past
few generations.

Every year we would weigh their horrendous mass on
the assumption that this told us something useful about
our ability to maintain stability in the world. But our
outcomes in the world seemed unrelated to that weight.

I suspect that students of correlation could learn
much more about our ability to influence the stability of

the world if they were to chart the acceptance in our population of some phrase like, "We are policemen to the world."

When the answer to that proposition was a naive "yes"—as it overwhelmingly was in the fifties—the United States was the strongest nation on earth.

When the answer in the sixties became a naive "no," it mattered not what our defense budget said. We were weak.

And when that condition coincided with North Vietnamese confidence—in blithe disregard of the laws of fire power—the result was Jericho.

In the late seventies we are much stronger, not because we merit it or because of our massive defense budgets, but because we have rebuilt a measure of our confidence that we will and can contribute to keeping some order in our world.

But at this writing a check with my neighbors suggests that the phrase "policeman to the world" still connotes more responsibility than we consider appropriate for our society.

This finding is not necessarily good news or bad news, but it is the type of information that is central to an understanding of our relative place in world power balances. Compared to this, the size of our defense establishment, or the course of our SALT diplomacy, is quite peripheral.

In this light, it looks as if many of our public policies may be misdirected, or at least not worth the effort. Meanwhile, our feelings and expectations about ourselves and our society seem to be sources of vastly greater power than we had credited to them.

The Media

When I worked as a newsman in the fifties, most of us sincerely believed that we could approximate an ideal of "objectivity" in selecting a few items from the flow of human affairs and deciding what to say about them.

A decade later many newsmen believed as earnestly in other ideals, such as "relevancy" or "advocacy."

If I were a newsman today, I might lean toward St. Paul's ideal—to "fill your minds with those things that are good and that deserve praise: things that are true, noble, right, pure, lovely and honorable."

The problem with any of these ideals is that a few people decide for the rest of society what is objective—or relevant—or what to advocate—or what St. Paul would have liked.

The lesson of the sixties is that the feelings and expectations that "fill our mind" can become Jericho, so we had better assume some personal responsibility for whatever goes into our minds. To leave that decision to a small profession that has had a tendency to run in a pack is a dangerous concentration of responsibility.

A simple way for a society to contain the power of the press is to define the news as being simply what the public will buy, and then for each of us to set high personal standards which the purveyors of news can try to satisfy.

This can give us trash, and no one to blame for it but ourselves. It can also give us what has become a recent blossoming of journals that focus on the positive rather than the negative aspects of human affairs.

Too Much News?

Another strategy is to reduce our intake of fast news.

Our fascination with the news and getting it fast goes back at least to Paul Revere. It probably reached a crest in the nineteen sixties. By then even the Oval Office was cluttered with terminals, including a three-screen TV console for the news-ravenous President. Television was at its peak, filling our homes with vivid images from around the world. Even as remote a place as my office in Vientiane boasted a small adjoining room with clattering news wires that I consulted often—so I could quickly inform the Ambassador of news developments.

In retrospect, the quality of the judgments throughout our society during those years seemed to decline as our access to information increased.

Finally, a corrective reaction began. In my case, I was so addicted to the pattern of incessant news that I had to quit completely for a while in order to realize that there were better ways to keep informed.

For me, the taste for TV news has never returned, and I hear radio news only by accident. A few times a week I scan a local paper, or flip through the Monitor. (It has the advantage of being a day late.) I usually skim one of the national news weeklies and read an occasional book on public affairs.

I like to spend a night in the squad car with my brother-in-law, a downtown Minneapolis police officer. This is a better police blotter than the media can offer—because the aberrations occur in the context of the utter boredom of most of the night—and because it reveals that cameraderie is much more the norm between people and the law than is confrontation.

Occasionally also I immerse myself in some affair of the politicians, or of the special interests and bureaucrats who influence the politicians, for a direct lesson in civics.

And I talk to my neighbors. Conversation, despite fears of its demise, is still alive in our society, and may even be growing. I have been kept informed by all sorts of people as we have conversed about our values or about the ways of our society. This book is a continuation of those conversations.

And there is silence. In our noisy determination to overcome loneliness, we have sometimes also drowned out silence, one of the great luxuries of our existence. Now we seem to be rediscovering it—in raspberry patches and other odd places. And a by-product of silence is a growing comprehension of the uncanny similarity between our internal states and the external world. Silence is an accurate way to know our world.

My own feeling is that I have a better understanding of the human condition these days than I did under the old regimen of reacting to the vividness of the electron media and the minutia of the print media.

I do not believe that people who have looked at pictures from Jonestown are better informed than the stout band who have not. It is not necessarily a copout to minimize human tragedy.

The creative way to be informed citizens is to stuff our minds with whatever it is we want to become the stuff of our realities. This is the lesson of Jericho, and of our recent history.

7
The Energy Blessing

Last summer we screened the porch. It was either that or install air conditioning, like we had in the old house, and we're glad we chose screening this time. The previous winter we had put in the wood stove and felt the quality of our life was improving. A few years back we adjusted to teasing a 55 mile-an-hour speed limit, rather than 65, and found our driving more enjoyable.

It is curious that these blessings all have roots in the energy crisis.

I can also name ways in which the crisis has hurt me. I recall, for example, the indignity of those lines at the gas pumps in 1974. But it is hard to think of many such incidents. I have been asking friends and people I meet how the energy crisis has hurt them, and they can't seem to think of much either.

A heresy beckons, but we will demur.

There are people, even in rich countries, for whom the spiralling cost of energy requires far more drastic adjustments than most of us make. Even for the more affluent, the added cost of energy could be calculated as money we might have used to stay out of debt, to drive a new car, or to eat less hamburger and more steak.

And yet—in our society all of this hardly adds up to a crisis that has taken a very bad turn. To say that it has would be to distort the natural adjustments that can benefit all of us, including the less affluent.

But maybe the real crisis is yet to come, deferred by the deft work of our politicians, and still a threatening catastrophe on the day when we actually scrape bottom in the oil barrels. It could then be harmful to let raspberry farmers and other assorted fools start pretending that we don't have a problem.

A worthy point.

On reflection, though, we realize that what the planners know is only that we are running out of cheap energy and will have to adapt accordingly. This fits the strict meaning of the word crisis, but not its negative connotation. What the planners cannot know is whether we will judge our adaptation to be a blessing or a curse or something else.

It is appropriate, then, to explore the delightful heresy that what mankind is now facing might be an "energy blessing."

Could it be that some of our ills can be blamed on the cheapness of our energy in relation to other costs? And if so, could it be possible that our lives might improve as the cost of energy increases in relation to other costs?

Technology in Balance

It would be folly to deny that technology has been a great blessing in most of our lives. Fueled by cheap energy, technology has vastly enlarged the range of choices that seem available to most of us.

But along with this marvelous liberation, technology also finds backhanded ways of trapping us into limiting and hurtful styles of living.

The balance between these two aspects of technology is a very delicate one, as a few examples will show:

Consider our jobs. Technology has tended both to raise the level of skill at which we work, and to limit its scope. It creates an enormous demand for people to work at a high level of skill. But it also competes with us for jobs. A chair made by a craftsman faces tough competition from the mass-produced model, manufactured and distributed with the use of cheap energy.

Or consider our cities. Cheap energy has enriched our urban civilization beyond anyone's dreams. Who foresaw a society in which almost every family would have a chariot or two? But the cheap energy that made this technology possible also helped to decay our cities. It became cheaper to live further out than to maintain a city. And as we sprawled, we fouled our air and imprisoned our commuters in steel for an hour or two a day.

Or consider our farms. Technology, with abundant cheap energy, has fired our productivity to the point where feeding the world needs to occupy only a small fraction of people's time and effort. But in the process the intricate cycles of farming are burning out. We are left with stinking feedlots, unfit for man or beast.

And consider our sense of community. With cheap energy we have blossomed into a global village. Our interdependencies range from ideas to oil. We can leave our car in an airport snowbank and be lounging on the beach two martinis later. But in the same process we have weakened our sense of engagement in meeting human needs—our own or those of others. A peasant would be horrified to learn that a human being could exist in such disharmony with his surroundings.

These balances between the blessing and the curse of our cheap energy technology are so delicate and so complicated that only a fool would dare try to adjust them. And the world has a few fools.

So, at times like the present, when many people feel the balances might be tilting a little more than they should be, our problem is not only what to do: We must also decide what fool should do it.

Tuning Technology

There are at least three candidates for the job of tuning our technology. It can be done by individuals, by societies, or by nature.

Tuning by individuals occurs through the myriad little market decisions each of us makes that, together, become the market principle. These decisions have served us fairly well in the past. They orchestrated the technological revolution, and they are now picking up the tune of our voluntary adjustments to simpler styles of living.

One of the problems with the market principle is that variations between individuals can be enormous, so that blessings like affluence or simplicity tend to be unevenly distributed. This can be bothersome to both the "haves" and the "have-nots" of a particular blessing.

Furthermore, even true believers in the market sometimes doubt whether the really big interdependent problems, like the spoiling of our environment, can be properly adjusted by the sum total of our individual self-interests.

Adjustments by society—the domain of our planners and politicians—have also served us fairly well in the past. Many people have felt that the benefits of our redistributions of resources in the Western democracies have more than offset the losses of individual freedom that resulted from collective action.

One problem with the planning process is that every adjustment a society makes seems to create unexpected ramifications, which then need further adjustment by more planners—and so forth, with no end in sight. This can be bothersome to both the planners, and their dwindling "plannees."

Furthermore, even true believers in social planning sometimes doubt whether planning can cope with the really enormous adjustments that may lie ahead for mankind.

What, for example, if the majority of us should really come to believe one day that the disadvantages of the private automobile outweighed its advantages? Who among us could weigh, or even identify, the myriad personal and global ramifications of adjusting for that?

Is this a job for a monorail mentality?

In the Western world for the past few centuries we have paid very little attention to the third agent of adjustment in our technology—namely nature. We have tended to think that excluding her from the play was the name of the game. Through private greed and collective bungling we have excluded her to the point where parts of the planet have become unlivable.

And now we are finding that neither private nor collective action may suffice to reverse the process. Here we have a legitimate use for the word crisis. It is our darkest hour.

But listen to those distant bugles!

The Energy Blessing

Galloping over the horizon, in the nick of time, comes the rescue party. It's the Energy Blessing! Call it nature or super-nature, an incredible piece of good luck or a *deus ex machina*—the marvel is that we are running out of cheap energy, and not a decade too soon.

So long as energy was so expendably cheap, it created disharmonies in our society which neither the market nor the planners seemed to be able to correct.

Nature's correction was to make energy a little harder to find. That changes all the equations. Suddenly it becomes easier for us to visualize a future in which there is a better balance between the benefit of technology and its backlash.

Now look again at those earlier examples.

Look at that hand-made chair. We can imagine it competing more successfully with the factory model. And from that we can project a renaissance of craftsmanship, and a decline in the number of people we meet who don't have work to do or who dislike the work they are doing. We can imagine a more costly technology concentrating on the tasks that humans really can't do as well alone, or really dislike doing.

Look at city life. With rising energy costs we will tend to find ways to reduce the distance between where we live and where we work. From such simple individual decisions, we can imagine our cities gradually rebuilding and thriving, and rush hour getting lighter every year, and the smog thinner. We can expect a welcome breath of diversity in our suburbs, as more people discover that double garages and walk-out basements are so well suited for home industry and professions. (In our own vicinity, four of our closest neighbors make their living at home, and this has helped make our neighborhood a strong and attractive model for the rest of the community.)

Look in the country. We can expect to see new roofs on those sagging barns. With rising energy costs the broken cycles of agriculture will heal, and the diversified family farm will resume its place as an efficient unit of agriculture. This is profoundly good news for civilization and for farmers.

Consider our sense of community. As work and home come closer together, we can expect a richer family life. With rising energy costs, the scale of our individual or collective undertakings will be less likely to ruin the planet. We can expect to feel more optimistic about the future of our civilization.

Seen in this light, there must be a more descriptive label than an "energy crisis" for the marvelous juncture our advanced technological societies seem to have reached.

The word crisis connotes that the outcome is in grave doubt. And in common usage it tends to carry the expectation that things will most likely turn out very badly.

Yet the likelihood in our case seems to be that we will look back on the drying up of cheap oil supplies as a great turning point, good for both mankind and the planet.

To christen so auspicious an event, we should reach for a noble name. This essay prefers "The Energy Blessing."

An Energy Principle

The exploration so far suggests that as the cost of energy increases in our society, the quality of life will improve. But there's more to it.

We can assume that there must be an upper range to those rising energy prices, where they would do us progressively less good and finally start hurting us more than they help us. This is similar to our experience at the other end of the scale, where cheap energy technology began yielding diminishing returns and eventually was doing us more harm than good.

This pattern suggests that there is an optimum range to a society's energy costs in relation to its other costs— at either end of which the quality of life seems to deteriorate.

This can be illustrated in both rich and poor settings.

Consider a North Asian peasant combing a denuded countryside for twigs to burn. His relative energy costs are unsatisfactorily high.

Consider a Western commuter locked in a smoggy traffic jam. His relative energy costs are unsatisfactorily low.

In between these extremes lie relative energy costs, at both affluent and simpler levels, that are likely to yield finer ways to live.

There are surely many variables that can put their dents in this design. For example, I cannot imagine a cheaper solar collector on my roof doing me or my society quite the damage a cheaper fossil fuel in my gas tank could. But I do not believe that such qualifiers will change the broad relationship we find between our relative energy costs and the quality of our lives.

Nor do I see a danger that the energy blessing will push our energy costs too high. There are many alternative sources of energy around, only modestly more expensive than the cheap fossil stuff, and there is lots of technology at hand for harnessing that energy.

What To do?

Now, if you confided to a politician that you had a simple little principle that would accomplish all these objectives, he might float to the ceiling for sheer joy. And if you added that the principle would work best if he did nothing about it, he would fall through the floor.

Do nothing? That's hard on most of us. Fortunately, whatever we do is not likely to do much long term harm. The energy blessing seems to be inevitable. Politicians and planners are not creating any new deposits of cheap fossil fuel. And, as more harmonious life styles become visible, more of us will tire of the disharmony of the old cheap energy ways.

So what should we do?

The following sections explore four possibilities. We can try to maintain the flow of cheap energy. We can try to be more fair about the distribution of available energy. We can try to reduce energy consumption. Or we can do nothing.

Maintain the Flow

We could keep trying, by public policy, to sustain the supply and contain the cost of energy. This is the bent of much of the energy policy that has filtered down to date. It has the advantage of delaying change. It can defer the energy blessing for a few years or a few decades.

After that, the imbalance resulting from cheap energy will have become more acute and harder to adjust. At that point, also, there will be less time for a smooth and natural adjustment to more satisfying life styles.

In this light, the objective of sustaining the flow of cheap energy makes little sense, especially for advanced technological societies like ours.

Only in less developed societies, that have not realized the diminishing returns of a cheap energy technology, might it be prudent for public policy to press development of new sources of energy—or to do mortal battle against the oil cartels.

Make It Fair

A second area of energy policy involves adjusting for the inequities of change. These can be windfall and shortfall inequities.

This area is the weak link in the market process, so it would be useful if it could be strengthened by public action. Unfortunately, it is also an area where our passions can easily interfere with our wisdom in designing a public policy.

The windfall question gnaws at me in odd moments, as it seems to gnaw at most people. Why should the big oil companies profit from all this? But neither I, nor any acquaintance of mine, has been sufficiently exercised to invest in oil stocks. The best that can be said is that most of our society's pension and retirement systems are heavily invested in oil.

In saner moments, I can see the windfall question as no more than a bothersome bagatelle in comparison with the promise of the energy blessing. Change is by nature uneven, so some windfall must be natural. If we nevertheless prefer to try moderating the windfall through public intervention, this should not distract us from broader goals.

And what about the shortfall? Many of us would dearly love to improve upon the limited ability of the market to be fair and even-handed in its distribution of scarcer and costlier energy. Alas, experience teaches that while planning often promises this benefit in theory, the market tends to deliver better in practice.

For example, I note that at the beginning of this essay the only hurt from an energy crisis that came to mind—those long lines at the gas pumps—resulted from planners trying to give me my fair share of gasoline.

In the more extreme instances of shortfall, we may still turn to public policy to help insure that some of these needs are met. But a thoughtful "plannee" will hardly expect such gains to spill over to the population at large.

A more promising approach to the shortfall question is the movement in our society toward forms of voluntary simplicity. This should take some of the sting out of living with less or more than our exact share of the world's energy and other material goodies.

Conserve Energy

A third possible area of energy policies would be the encouragement of more prudent use of energy in our society. This could speed the arrival of the energy blessing, and is probably a worthy goal. But it is unlikely that any of us could design a smoother transition to the energy blessing than what nature has designed by imposing on the market an end to cheap fossil fuels.

Given our American penchant for improving on a good thing, though, we can assume that a spreading awareness of the energy blessing will spur horrendous efforts to hurry its coming. This could do some harm, and it might even do a little good.

In particular, I think it will become important for us to start dismantling some of the energy wasting horrors that we have built into our public sector. This needs deliberate doing because the public sector is not well equipped to respond spontaneously to market influences.

Consider, for example, the gross overspecification of most public construction in relation to equivalent private construction. Add to this the fact that most private construction is grossly overspecified in order to conform to public codes and policies.

In our community recently we encountered a typical specimen of such horrors. The discussion concerned a projected freeway extension that would block access to a small pocket of land containing a few dozen homes along a lake. A bridge over the freeway seemed a possible solution. I had visions of something quaint, maybe even a one-lane connection, such as those that join the lovely little residential islands in the Oslofjord. Alas, a discussion with the highway people revealed that the smallest bridge our engineers could squeeze out of their specifications was 44 feet wide.

Do Nothing

In the private sector the easiest and most natural energy policy, if we had the nerve for it, would be to allow our individual market decisions to adjust to nature's marvelous intervention.

With nature's incentive, we would find ourselves shaping our individual self-interests into nicer ways to live and into greater harmony with global interests. It is very hard to imagine a planned social intervention that could improve on this simple model.

For many of us, unfortunately, it is much more complicated than that. With Walt Whitman we must say, "I contain multitudes!"

Only in our better moments can we welcome the natural unfolding of an energy blessing.

At more mundane times, change is the enemy. We prefer what we know, even though we recognize the disharmony of it.

At still other times, our paranoia takes the upper hand, so we guard our private stakes in cheap energy while fighting off the other exploiters.

A machine is always more cumbersome than the mind that made it. The machinery of a society is no exception. Our bureaucrats and politicians have difficulty responding to a vague and evolving consensus, like the notion of an energy blessing. The machinery prefers to deal with our more crass concerns, like windfalls and shortfalls, and such simple wishes as "Change, change, go away. Come again another day."

But once man decides what he wants from his machine, he applies his inventiveness to make it do his will. This is such a time for the machinery of our society.

Summary

It appears that many of the ills of a highly technological society like ours can be blamed on the relative cheapness of our energy. Neither private nor public policy seems able to cure these ills. But nature, by making energy a little harder to find, is creating the impetus for a transition to more harmonious ways of living.

The energy blessing suggests that a broad principle is at work, in both rich and poor societies: there is an optimum range to a society's energy costs, relative to its other costs, at either end of which the quality of life seems to deteriorate.

The energy blessing is inevitable, unfolding naturally through the action of higher energy costs on market processes. Public policy will have only modest effect, for good or ill, on this transition.

8
The Inner Sector

It seems to me that there is a common theme in these essays and in many of the other explorations of how to live and think that are underway in our society. It is the feeling that we must look more to our inner selves and less to our external resources for the qualities we want in our lives.

The consequences of this insight are primarily personal ones. That has been the case throughout history.

But as more of us move in this direction, even by small subtle moves, the theme shows up in the way our society works and colors our common understanding of concepts like community and compassion.

I think we are in the process of expanding a category that could be called the Inner Sector.

Into this sector we are transferring some large hunks of the expectations we used to house in old external categories of the Private Sector and the Public Sector. This process may illuminate why Wall Street can't get past the one thousand mark on the Dow Jones Industrials, and why the sentiment to cut back our public sector runs so deep in many of us.

Consider some of the remarkable changes going on in the way we live and think:

The Unspecialist

Diplomats create foreign policy; educators develop curricula, engineers design highways; and doctors decide how to treat disease. They often do a good job. For centuries it was our habit to honor the ever-narrowing specializations of our technological societies.

But diplomats gave us Vietnam, educators gave us "Johnny can't read," engineers gave us overspecification, and doctors gave us excuses for getting sick. We are finally realizing that there are limits to the blessing of specialization.

The new ideal is the unspecialist, an individual or a society that draws on expert advice as desired, and then designs and takes responsibility for a course of action that is judged to be consistent with the inner sector's sense of wholeness. Ultimately, only the client knows what he wants in Vietnam, or what his children should learn, or how wide he wishes his highway to be, or whether he will be healed.

All of us are specialists in something or other. So it is not surprising that most of us would like to exclude the unspecialist barbarians from those little domains that we understand better than others. (e.g., Vietnam should have been done my way.)

But our dependencies have far exceeded our special skills, and in all the other little domains the specialists seem to have burdened us with expertise that we have not asked for.

So we are delighted that it is now considered good form to question the advice of an expert. We will even admit the barbarians to our own domains in return for the chance to groom our inner selves into stronger, more confident unspecialists at the whole of life.

We can expect this trend to continue. We still have quite far to go to achieve a good balance between the responsibilities of the client and of his experts.

I believe, for instance, that peer review in the trades and professions will end up having a rather parochial meaning within any given field, and that the substantive measure of a specialist will become the extent to which he meets the needs of his clients. As we move in this direction, we will have a declining need for the services of trade and professional organizations and government regulators.

And our inner sectors will grow.

The Unminority

Our society has recently sustained a generation of intense awareness of our minority loyalties. We have learned something about the strengths and weaknesses of this mode of improving upon ourselves and society.

We began the generation nobly enough with the civil rights movement of black Americans. We ended it in exhaustion with what had become a cacophony of segmented "rights" and demands for affirmative action.

By then we even had a men's movement, one of whose earnest leaders once suggested that I write something about househusbandry for their "survival manual." I had to decline on grounds that I was a person, not a man!

It startles us now to recall that the proud "I have a dream" of Martin Luther King was the antithesis of the later segmentation. His dream was integration. His was a dream to end the labeling of minorities, a dream to end the movement.

Our family has no particular shortage of limiting minority labels, and we have had to think about how much of our identity we will invest in them.

In my case, I could have polarized around being an ex-POW, an immigrant, a super-patriot, a Republican, a newsman, a Christian, a foreign service officer, or "just a househusband."

My wife could have identified herself as an unsophisticated, mid-western farm girl, a research scientist, a practicing pediatrician, or as an oppressed career woman in a male chauvinist world.

Our kids could think of themselves as "different" since they have no color TV and their parents don't even assume the usual family roles. Besides, two of them are adopted—one an Asian with a flat nose—the other a mixture of Black, Native American and German, with curly hair. In the old jargon, the school psychologist would rush to flag our family as being "at risk."

But things are changing.

As the Inner Sector grows there is evolving a consensus about the nature both of our minority identifications and our majority ones. To cling to any of them, or to reject any of them, is by definition limiting to the growth of the whole. The ideal starts with accepting openly and proudly any label that fits. And then we ignore it. The goal is to push our loyalties into as broad a set of identifications as we can muster, and to keep expanding them whenever we can make a broader label fit.

In our family we occasionally make a nice fuss about one of the racial origins we encompass. We are saving for a return trip to Asia and Africa. And a few summers ago we traced Karen's roots to the Sognefjord, where she milked cows in the ancestral barn.

But we try not to go overboard on the Sons of Norway mystique or their counterparts in the races of our children.

If things work as we hope they will, our children will sense as a matter of course what our generation has to work at sensing—that we are citizens of Earth.

Movements Hinder

As specialists or as minorities, as seekers of narrow economic goals or as advocates of broad political causes, we all end up riding a movement. And a movement is the antithesis of the inner sector. The movement is a crowd polarized around a segment of life. The inner sector is intimate and rooted in the whole of life.

Movements can turn us into single issue voters, and reduce our democratic process to a free-for-all between special interest groups.

The alternative is so subtle that we rarely remember to use it, and when we do we are hardly aware of it.

In the mid-seventies American society used it on a massive scale. After "the sixties" and Vietnam and Watergate our national sense of esteem and confidence had fallen drastically. Our opinion leaders generally were offering little hope of a worthier tomorrow. Where would it all end?

Imperceptibly, a quiet segment of our population began reversing that prognosis.

When we moved to Minnesota in 1974 from a demoralized Washington, we were startled by the simple impression that civilization here was still intact. The headlines were as dreary as out east—but the people were not.

The heartland had quietly decided that the dream would be believable again. You could cash a check in the grocery store; you could lean on the service industries and get answers, not excuses. Then we looked again on the coast and saw that it was happening there too, very subtly. I remember the immaculate lobby I entered on a tattered rental block. Someone there believed.

It helped that Mr. Ford and later Mr. Carter believed. But there were few optimists among our visible opinion makers.

Quietly one morning the accumulation of small beliefs burst into a new national consensus. It was our bicentennial Fourth of July in 1976. It happened suddenly and without any movement to push us. We just knew that we were ready to celebrate the turning point in our crisis. We would recover.

The force behind that recovery had been enormous. But it had never been a movement. It was a work of the inner sector.

It grieves me that I should have this insight and still be as prone as I am, at small provocations, to mount a movement and go riding off to some pole or other. At our higher levels of awareness we know that the goals we seek are achieved if we can pursue them as works of the inner sector.

Materialism

The decline of materialism in our society is probably more real than apparent.

At the daily level we still huff and puff about meeting material ends—stretching family budgets, harnessing the public sector, and planning for global shortages.

At a slightly different level of awareness we sense an opposite problem—the feeling that our advanced technological societies may be reaching the point of diminishing returns in their pursuit of material well-being.

Most of us believe, I think, that this second view represents our higher aspiration, and we feel it quietly growing.

My raspberry patch is a tiny example of the countless bits of material illogic that have become part of our society's exploration of new options, something more satisfying than just increasing the standard of living. As the market reflects these non-economic pursuits of happiness, we can expect our economies to decline and our inner sectors to grow.

Consider what all this does to the spectrum of values that belong to that venerable sacred cow of our value system—materialism.

On the right, it threatens our material success ethic, which has dominated our thinking since the industrial revolution and stunted our spiritual growth.

On the left, it threatens all the hoary rhetoric of "haves" and "have nots" that has powered so many of our political, social and religious movements in recent centuries.

All these values can safely recede, I think, without endangering either our capacity to get a day's work out of ourselves, or our capacity to be compassionate about each other's weaknesses.

Spreading the Wealth

I think we can expect the accumulation of great wealth to decline as a very attractive goal in life (and to yield faster if we continue to see so much evidence around that a large inheritance can be such a poor legacy to leave our children).

If it goes far enough, we might even begin regarding the rich as disadvantaged, as Jesus taught in the parable of the camel and the needle's eye.

While we wait for that utopia, though, it remains a fact that most of us have a strong distaste for extreme concentrations both of wealth and of scarcity. They are disruptive to a society.

Admittedly, we have done a better job of spreading

the wealth than most countries. But there is more to do.

In the public sector we are hindered by a clumsy tax law, and by the tendency of our politicians and bureaucrats to spend the money rather than distribute it.

In the private sector our high technology generates a lot of wealth, but it creates relatively few productive jobs. So the weak link is the mechanism for distributing the wealth.

We could keep trying to contrive more jobs for our population. We could shuffle more papers. China has used this strategy—ending unemployment by overstaffing the state-run economy. Surely a more elegant and liberating solution can be found, possibly through some direct method of spreading the wealth.

With the decline of materialism helping to free us from yesterday's polarizing influences, it should be easier to find that more elegant answer. And that would be a worthy task for our external sectors.

Quality of Life

It may still be true that there is more poverty among those of us with few material resources than among those of us with many of them.

But the contradictions in that simple old assumption are mounting fast. There are just too many people, like my mother-in-law, living splendid lives at a near subsistence level. And most of us are aware, in ourselves and in others, of periods of tragic need amid relative material wealth.

Clearly an urgent act of compassion in our society is to find a way to measure the quality of our lives in terms other than material ones. Until we do, some of us who need a brother's help will be excluded from it by definition. And others of us will have our lives cheapened by being offered a form of compassion we do not need.

"Yes, but," we want to say—and we want to add a lower limit of acceptable material scarcity.

Where to peg that limit varies with every society, suggesting that it is a relative limit, not an absolute one. The extent of this relativity can be hard for a society to understand.

For example, even mild levels of chronic hunger, such as I experienced during the teenage years in a prison camp, are difficult to comprehend in our society. Very few people here have experienced it, and our culture simply assumes that it should be a perfectly awful experience.

Yet much of the world's population goes to bed slightly hungry most nights.

This chronic malnutrition in some societies is fairly analogous to the chronic obesity that characterizes ours. Both states are unhealthy, slightly shameful, and zealously to be avoided if one can manage it. But in each society we learn to cope somehow with one state or the other. And there are always a few ascetics or cherubs around who make a virtue out of the deficiency.

But come now!

What about the starvation level? We would insist on drawing a line above that. But even as we do, we ponder the evidence being weighed by people like my wife in the field of international medicine. It seems that even the most dread diseases of severe malnutrition are associated, not only with nutritional deficiencies, but also with

118

other factors that can contribute to stress.

The state of our material resources is not the only misleading indicator of quality in our lives.

Another one is the level of our adversities. Granted, the preference for an easy life is nearly universal. Yet, when we look back on our difficulties, we often see them as sources of enrichment in our lives.

A friend of ours, whose family raised two retarded children at home, says they lived the task as a rich and unifying experience. Occasional articles in my wife's medical journals speak of a category called "the invulnerable child" for those who in spite of calamities mature into splendid adults.

The only meaningful way I have found to think about the quality of our lives is in terms of the quality of the dreams that surround each of us. Our expectations of life, both good and bad, seem to have an inner power that far outweighs any external influences on us.

If this is so, we can think of compassion as something that contributes to the quality of another's dream. And how do we do that?

A Health Model

When I was a pre-schooler in Northwest China, the nearest Western doctor was seven days' journey away, by mule. None of us was ever sick enough to see him. (The doctor was Walter Judd, the medical missionary who later became a Minnesota congressman.)

When we went to boarding school on the coast, they had a staff physician. I was a rather sickly child with chronic boils and sometimes needed hospitalization.

In prison camp medical facilities were very limited and almost none of us got sick. As an immigrant to America, I had neither time nor resources for sickness. I even survived a stint in the Army where care would have been free.

My exposure to fairly comprehensive health insurance began when I worked for the U.S. Congress in the late fifties. That's when I had surgery for an abscess, and a bout with pneumonia.

Then I joined USIA and encountered the Embassy Doctor. I even married one. I had amoebic dysentery, and hemorrhoids, and an intestinal polyp, and an NIH work-up for tropical sprue. I fractured my back and heel, and progressed slowly from hospital bed to wheelchair to crutches.

Then I broke my back again.

By this time I was finally understanding myself well enough to call my own bluff. This triggered a crisis of the inner sector, and an access to grace that had me on my feet the next day.

I have had to conclude that I get sick and get well when it suits me—which is a lovely thought when I am well, and an ugly one when I am not.

Looking back now on the first fracture and the months it took to recover, I recognize several forms of compassion that came my way.

One was pity: It comforted me and made me feel better about my dependence.

Another was "caring"—my wife giving backrubs or emptying the commode, and later my co-worker coming by every morning to take me and my wheelchair to work.

A third form of compassion was the refusal of my wife

and our friends to think of my condition as anything but a temporary aberration.

In retrospect, the pity slowed my recovery. The caring eased it. And the expectation of friends cured me.

These sorts of insights are now fairly common in our society. Most of us are not yet prepared to take them all the way to their logical conclusion. But we are moving in the direction of taking more personal responsibility for our health and the condition of our lives.

The health industry is changing with us. My wife and many of her colleagues like to think of themselves in the role of coaches, showing clients how to live healthier lives and how to facilitate healing.

Nung and Song

The Southeast Asian refugees settling in Minnesota during the past few years have been the source of special friendships for us, both because we knew some of them in Laos, and because they are a vivid reminder of my own introduction to America.

I had lots of help in 1946. Our tickets were furnished by the Red Cross, and we were dressed from a blue bag full of clothes that had been issued to each of us. A remote uncle had signed the affadavit that I would not become a financial burden to this country. Other relatives and church friends offered housing, jobs and moorings.

They were also living reminders that they themselves had been immigrants and were now self-sufficient. They soon coaxed me out of their nest.

Nung was a French-trained agronomist from Laos who came to Minneapolis as a refugee. Local church groups helped each refugee family get settled and started.

I went job hunting with Nung. A local seed company offered him a job—on the assembly line. Nung swallowed his pride and took it. I was confident that another dream had been launched. We had little contact after that. I heard that he was laid off for a while, but since he did not call me, I assumed he was solving the problem.

Students of Asian "face" and American "dreams" will relish the appropriateness of Nung's visit to our house last spring.

He was now, he said, in the company's sugar beet research program and they were looking for additional experimental plots in a variety of soils. Would I consider renting them a small patch of land? It was the sweetest $25 I ever made. Our friendship grew as we nursed that plot through the summer.

And Nung told me the startling parable of his big break with the seed company.

It had started with his lay-off. When he went looking for another job, a prospective employer called the old company, where someone pulled Nung's file, took a second look at those credentials and said, "No—we need him back!"

Another friend was Song, who had been an aircraft mechanic in Laos. This was a rare talent in that country, but his license meant little when he and his family arrived here as refugees.

We got him a job cleaning engine parts for a local airline. The pay was good. In less than a year Song had become the first of his group of refugees to buy a car, and not long after he was asking for advice on buying a home.

I decided to ignore the conventional gloom in social planning circles over the fact that much of our metropolitan population can no longer afford to buy housing. If a house was what he wanted, I told him, he had only to signal the vaguest interest to any real estate agency, and they would stretch his available downpayment and income as far as anyone could stretch it in the housing market.

On his own Song struck a deal with two thousand down for a $29,000 house. I helped at the closing and saw the ecstasy in the whole family at having become property owners in their new land.

Then came the pilots' strike, and Song was laid off, along with thousands of others making a fraction of pilot's pay.

The mortgage company was only a small problem; a phone call took care of that.

The big problem was Song's circle of friends. Every time I urged him to get another job, some of them would tell him that doing so would be a terrible mistake, since it could mess up his unemployment checks. Song got confused. He took a job, quit a week later, lost his unemployment and grieved to learn that I could not intercede with the employment office.

The church helped him through. And he fished for some of his food until he found another job. Finally, the airline called him back. Now he's talking about trading up for a bigger house. And he took his family on a Hawaiian vacation.

An Institution

If we must at times create institutions in the name of

compassion, the strengths of a place like the Minneapolis Children's Health Center are well worth noting. The dream that created this unique hospital was what enticed us five years ago to move from Washington to Minneapolis.

The dream was of a place where the needs of the clients—children—would take precedence over the needs of the institution and all the health care workers.

It incubated for several decades in the minds of a few professionals and a lot of mothers. An annual bazaar began raising a few hundred dollars a year, then a few thousand, and now it raises hundreds of thousands. The hospital was built in the early seventies, entirely with private contributions. It cost about $4.5 million. Comparable hospitals built with public funding in other cities were costing more than ten times that amount.

Walking down the hall from the elevators you approach not a nursing station, but a play room. A mental health ecology program works at helping everyone who will encounter the children to be sensitive to the totality of their needs. From the colored smocks to the closed-circuit TV programs, this is a place for children.

The education program here is aimed at helping students and professionals learn to treat the whole child.

Even the research has a unique flavor. Most of it is locally funded. The accountability is not to some distant bureaucracy, but to a group of mothers in someone's house who have an intimate stake in where the state-of-the art is taking us.

Compassion

The preceding sections are illustrative of one person's

experience with receiving compassion, trying to offer it, and seeing it work in an institution.

I do not pretend to understand compassion, and I hope to improve upon the limited sense of it I may think I have. But my experience so far suggests this:

Much of the compassion we share has to do with raising the quality of one another's dreams. It seems to have little to do with the rearranging of external resources that have become associated with the word.

A person who makes me aware of how much control I have over my outcomes is offering me compassion.

And a person who will lend me his imagination, expecting for me a happy outcome that I cannot quite conjure up in myself—that person is truly "visiting the orphans and widows in their affliction."

Community

Next door to us live the old raspberry farmers, both in their late seventies. He has trouble walking, and she is often in pain. In our weaker moments we wonder how they stay self-sufficient in the old farm house. But they do. And on some bitter cold mornings the old man is the only one around who can get a car started, and then he lets us borrow it. Occasionally, a neighbor will help them plow the driveway or run them on an errand that is off their familiar routes. But mostly we just have good times together or leave each other alone.

The rest of this exurban neighborhood is equally improbable.

Our yards range from busy ones, cluttered with trucks and equipment, to manicured lawns that would make the suburbs blush. We have both an epidemic of

Canadian thistle and a truck farmer whose perfect toma-
to stakes run straighter than the crosses at Arlington
Cemetery. We have young couples just starting families
and retired farmers. We have businessmen and assem-
blyline workers and professional people, and even a peri-
patetic househusband pretending to be a raspberry
farmer.

To our delight, and to the puzzlement of the external
sectors, we are a neighborhood—in fact a strong and co-
hesive one.

The private sector wishes we were more impatient for
the day when this whole mess might become worth tear-
ing down for development.

The public sector is digesting the incongruity that we
have become a neighborhood without benefit of the
planning, homogenizing and servicing that neighbor-
hoods are supposed to require.

What is probably happening is that our neighborhood is evolving toward some new ideal of community.

Ever since societies like ours lost their extended families, we have been looking for a replacement. We tried
delegating our interdependencies to a large and imper-
sonal public sector and found that unworkable. We tried
banding into narrow homogeneous groups and found
that too limiting.

Now we seem to be coalescing into more diverse little
communities, in which our strengths and weaknesses
complement each other better. These mixed groupings
are more consistent with the expanding identities we are
beginning to assume in our societies and our world. And
they harmonize with our discovery of a much wider
range of external indicators of the good life in our world.

If the private developers and the public planners can be a little bit patient, I think our neighborhood might end up being remembered as an early example of a renaissance community.

9
Miracles

"And with all thy getting, get understanding."
King Solomon

In heavy traffic I tend to be a lane switcher. But sometimes I play a little game instead.

First, I fill my mind with the expectation that the Law of Averages is in superb working order today. And sure enough, that yellow car on my left will hover for miles within a few car lengths of mine.

Then I invoke Murphy's Law. I fill my mind with the expectation that if anything can possibly go wrong with the speed of the traffic in my lane, it will. I rarely stay long voluntarily in that state of mind, because the law proves itself so promptly.

Then I invoke Torjesen's Law. If anything can possibly go right, it will. This state of mind may be slightly harder to get into than the others, because many of us are programmed to think like scientists—or losers.

But all three states of mind are on the same spectrum. And all three laws work.

The trouble with this boisterous game is that we play it on the neat turfs of two of the more venerable institutions on earth—science and religion. One is arbiter of natural laws and the other of miracles. Since many of us think of ourselves as being both scientific and religious, we had better find a more respectful way to enter these grounds.

Verse might be appropriate.

Science and Religion

"It's in the Data!"

"It's in the Word!"

Purebred modes of thought

that bareback vault their riders

clear to truth.

But in Dogma's harness,

each hauls freight

to ignorance.

The Data

Science has been having the same problem the Church was having in the Middle Ages—it has been the only show in town. So it has become rather dogmatic and set in its ways. Magnificent intellectual abstractions—atoms and molecules for example— suffered the fate of earlier marvels like confession and atonement. They become fixed entities in the minds of all but the more imaginative of men.

But imagination survived in Science, as it did in the Church. Heisenberg, for example, feels that every particle consists of all other particles, and holds to a concept of fundamental symmetry, rather than one of fundamental particles.*

To a wide-eyed bystander, it seems that another Copernican revolution is rumbling in our century, with the heresy this time being an attempt to expend our system of reality to encompass both matter and mind, both the "out there" and the "in here" of what we experience.

Admittedly, our run-of-the-mill scientists still prefer to design "double blind" experiments that try to *exclude* the mind factor rather than *integrate* it. And their results still appeal to us, as indulgences appeal in their day.

But the new consciousness is capturing imaginations both in science and in the laity, and it looks like things are beginning to change fairly fast.

How we will look tomorrow I do not know. Maybe even as hallowed a dogma as the belief that a valid experiment must be repeatable will end up in the quaint

---

*Gerald Holton, *The Scientific Imagination*, Cambridge, 1978, pp. 18-20.

category with the pre-Copernican notion that our earth is the center of the cosmos.

But science, like the church, will survive, and thrive.

The Word

Thoretically, religion should be delighted with the emerging concepts of reality. They reaffirm what all the great teachers have said.

I was brought up on the teachings of Jesus. These are his words:

"As a man thinketh in his heart, so is he."

"All things are possible to him that believeth."

"If ye have faith as a grain of mustard seed, ye shall say unto this mountain, Remove hence to yonder place; and it shall remove; and nothing shall be impossible unto you."

But there are difficulties for religion in all this.

During the several hundred years that miracles were out of fashion in good scientific company, the tendency in religious circles was to finesse the subject and find other things to talk about.

Even today a person who discovers himself miraculously in the fastest lane of traffic on the freeway will not necessarily look to his religion as the context in which to understand the experience.

My missionary mother told a piercing tale about an old Chinese peasant woman who discovered the mustard seed story and decided to take mountain-moving literally.

The woman lived in Northwest China during the

Sino-Japanese War in a town near the front lines that regularly changed hands between Japanese, Nationalist and Communist troops. Across a steep hill from her house stood my parents' mission church. A zealous convert, the lady spent hours every Sunday limping over the mountain and back on her old-fashioned bound feet to attend church.

Then she decided to move the mountain. Mother was awed by her faith, but she also wanted to prepare the dear lady for the possibility that "God's will" for that particular mountain might differ from hers.

At about this time the Japanese occupiers began building military fortifications in the hillsides. Then suddenly they abandoned the town. What they left behind was a nice, straight tunnel from the lady's house to the church.

It has been hard in our culture—even in religious circles—to digest a story like that. But it is becoming easier. There is a growing realization that what we sense inside is reflected outside.

What's so special about a mustard seed?

When we contemplate the seed, we realize the one special thing about it is its imprinting to be a mustard tree and nothing else. Not a cell in that kernel harbors any sense of turning out to be anything else on earth than a mustard tree. Even if the seed ends up flavoring a ham-on-rye it continues to express the essence of a mustard tree and nothing else.

We share with the mustard seed the deep sense that our expectations unfold into our reality. We differ from the mustard seed only in our freedom to choose what those expectations will be.

"My Revelation"

Another problem with religion, and with the analysis above, is that most of us are fixated on our own revelation of "the word," either as we have derived it from our particular tradition or experienced it directly. The human tendency is to think of all other revelations as somehow suspect.

"Will all miracles please observe the requirement to occur within the context of my revelation!"

When we cannot make miracles observe this rule, we prefer to discount them. (Science has the same problem.)

The institutions of religion will need to get over this intolerance, or lose their claim to miracles, just as they lost their claim to knowledge in the last renaissance.

Individually, we have the same task—to transcend the feeling of exclusiveness about our own "my revelation."

But once we abandon those limits to miracles, the "my revelation" tends to become more meaningful than ever. It then becomes natural and appropriate to pursue the new reality in the context of whatever has been our own tradition.

For me the word "prayer" describes precisely the process by which I quiet myself and open a new reality. That word has lived in me since childhood and is permeated with meaning.

I have no need to adopt an Eastern or humanistic or scientific terminology. Those are worthy vocabularies serving other revelations and blessed with meaning for others.

For me, when my mind is filled, inexplicably, with

the certainty of a new reality, then a term like "born again" offers a vivid image of that access to grace.

Grace

The creation of new expectations seem to take place in our consciousness. But the more we force them, the more they evade us.

The process apparently occurs beyond the domain of our own egos. When we offer a miracle to another, we heal ourselves. When our minds reach past the limits of the ego, we sense an infinite grace. At this point insert a homily from your own tradition.

"Underneath are the everlasting arms."

Creation

The implications of the new reality can be quite overwhelming in our world. But they are positive. And they are unfolding rather slowly, so we can adjust—individually and in our institutions.

The questions to ask ourselves in the present are these: What outcome do I want? Is my expectation of myself and of my society equal to what I want for an outcome?

My first answer to such questions is a limiting one. I want and expect some order in my universe. Most of us seem to need that. Most of us, most of the time, believe in the natural laws; and because of the consensus on this, many things in our world are rather predictable. A scientist can still stake his reputation on the scientific method. And a gambler can still live by the roll of the dice.

I remember the time I tested that last truth. I was a GI in Europe in the fifties. Striding into the Monte Carlo in Monaco, I put down enough francs to buy one lonely chip. "That's all I need," I confided to the jaded cashier. I placed it on my overwhelming hunch, number 27. Seconds later it was gone.

The consensus in our world is that games of chance will be governed by chance. Dents in that consensus are very small indeed. Were it otherwise, we would redesign the dice.

Within these reassuring limitations, we can expect to increase our freedom to choose and to change our outcomes a step at a time. And along with that freedom we will also increase our sense of personal responsibility for our individual outcomes and those of our world.

The point of power in a healthy person is always the present. Our genes and our experiences may contribute to what we expect of ourselves and each other. But they need not dominate it. We can do much better or much worse than that. If our personal realities do not satisfy us, we can change them to whatever extent we are able to change our expectation of ourselves and of each other.

All of this can seem to load an enormous freedom and responsibility on each of us for our outcomes, both individual and collective. How far can it go? For most of us there is a point beyond which we dare not go. It is a point we may move ahead a few notches tomorrow, but it must stay today where each of us puts it. There is still a vast distance between us and the man who looked at a jar of water and saw wine.

"Greater works than these shall ye do."

Precise Reality

When I expect
my world to follow solid lines
of fact and truth,
you oblige.

When I lapse
to feel it fettered to chance,
or bound to go wrong,
you conform.

And when I rise
to name you equal to my fondish wish,
you carve my dream
in your very flesh.

I understand so little
about you, reality,
except that you honor my feelings
precisely.

Conclusion

Each of us pursues a separate exploration of ways to live and think, and we make different turns along the way. Obviously, only one person could muddle into the particular combination of attitudes expressed in these essays.

It is curious, though, that this exploration seems to have ended up in the same general area where so many explorations, starting from so many places, seem to be ending up, namely at a confluence of our inner and outer realities. There must be some new synthesis in the works.

This exploration confirms what other explorers have found: that whenever we accept an opportunity for change in one area of our lives—for example in the trading of family roles—it tends to have a ripple effect that opens new choices in other areas of our living and thinking that may have seemed fixed. The ripples around here are still shimmering, suggesting interesting days ahead.

Here are some personal conclusions:

It works to trade family roles.

All aspects of my life are interrelated, so that my understanding of the kitchen sink equates with my understanding of myself or my cosmos.

Dogmas are not binding in my style of living or in my scientific or religious or political thinking or in any other area of my life.

But I keep them as long as I like.

Once I decide to dissolve one little dogma, lots of other stereotypes of my living and thinking open up to revision.

I revise these at whatever pace I find comfortable.

But it helps to burn some bridges behind me.

The more stereotypes I dissolve, the more I find.

Therefore every idea in this book is so very tentative and transitional.

My external reality reflects the feelings, images and expectations that constitute my inner state, and those of others that I accept.

I change external reality by changing my inner state.

This is prayer. It is a work of grace, not of the ego.

The nicest way to live and think is to spend life exploring ways to live and think.

ORDER FORM

Mail this order to:

THE GARDEN
P.O. Box 844
Eden Prairie, Minnesota 55344

Enclosed is $_____ for ____ copies of THE HOUSEHUSBAND'S WORLD, at $3.95 each, plus 50 cents for postage and handling.

(Quantity discounts available. Prices subject to change without notice.)

SHIP TO:

NAME _____

ADDRESS_____

_____

_____